Real moms encouraging moms to know the love of Christ

Dearest friend,

In your hands you are holding an invitation to grow steadfast in your walk with this Lord this summer! *The Wise Woman Stays* devotional workbook will encourage you on your journey to stay committed to your husband, remain engaged with your children, stay connected to the body of Christ, and be a dedicated friend. Most importantly, you will learn to stay close to God, unwavering in your relationship with Him even when times get tough. Satan wants you to throw in the towel on your faith, marriage, and family, but the Bible says you will reap a harvest if you do not give up (Galatians 6:9).

One of the most beautiful things about being a Christ follower is having the power of the Holy Spirit living inside of you. Because Jesus overcame sin, we can overcome struggles in this life as well! God wants you to remain faithful to His calling on your life, and through His Word He will equip you to do so. We are so thankful you have decided to join our band of real, ordinary moms as we journey together in God's Word and seek to have our best, most life-changing summer ever!

There are three important components in this study, each designed to encourage you in your roles as a Christian woman, wife, and mother:

Prayer: We believe prayer changes everything, and we encourage you to prayerfully consider finding someone with whom you can pray once a week over the phone, preferably someone who is doing this Bible study as well. This one habit of praying with a prayer partner will change your life!

Bible Study: Included in your workbook each week are four Bible studies to encourage and inspire you to remain steadfast in life! Each study begins with Scripture to read and meditate on, which will prepare you to fellowship with your beautiful Savior. The studies always end with "Go Deeper" and "What's Next" sections. These are meant to stir your heart and mind into action and to bring lasting, godly change to your everyday life! We hope you will be drawn into a deeper relationship with our Heavenly Father as you actively pursue intimacy with Him. May the foundational truths you discover anchor you as you stay faithful to Jesus!

Mom Tips: We are so excited to share our Mom Tips with you each week! These practical ideas are meant to enhance your life as a Christian wife, mom, discipler of your children, homemaker, and friend. You can pray about which tips to try, and you can check them off as you accomplish them. Feel free to just work on one tip or to complete them all as you are able!

We pray this Summer of Staying will be an amazing turning point for you as God grows you into the strong, immovable believer, wife, mother, and friend He has called you to be! Allow the Lord to satisfy your heart this summer and fill you with His joy and peace. He has great plans for you! Let's walk this road of faithfulness together sisters!

Blessings and love,

The Help Club for Moms Team

The Wise Woman Stays

What does it mean to stay?

In a culture that is fast-paced, on the go, and pushing change, this idea can be lost. As moms, our "jobs" in our home can feel mundane at best and our hearts long for change and a new rhythm from time to time. The concept of staying is often one that comes with a bit of resistance. For example:

- How do you *stay* when the journey ahead looks murky and unclear? Even hopeless?

- How do you *stay* when someone has been unfaithful or has hurt you deeply?

- How do you *stay* when you feel as though you are stuck in a hamster wheel and are going nowhere? Whether in a relationship or life in general?

- How do you *stay* when a friendship feels complicated and disappointing?

- How do you *stay* and remain in love when your child is continually disobedient and disrespectful?

- How do you *stay* when you feel as though God has not answered prayers and doesn't seem to hear your cries for help?

...there are many more circumstances in life that make the idea of staying so difficult, but friends, it is the way.

In 2 Timothy 4:7 it says, "I have fought the good fight, I have finished the race, I have kept the faith."

Mom, in order to fight the good fight and to finish the race, we must persevere when the going gets tough. There are a million reasons to quit. Culture and Satan will tempt you with the grass being greener on the other side of your circumstance. It takes courage to stay when you have been deeply hurt, It takes perseverance to push through a job that seemingly yields no fruit but pays the bills. It takes bravery to embrace someone you love after they have betrayed you. It takes boldness to step out in faith and pray again and again after what feels like silence on the other side.

Our obedience in staying when the going gets tough is what builds our faith and produces the character and person that God created us to be! It is the refining power that will truly help make the "grass feel greener" right where you are.

Jesus gave us such a beautiful example of staying. When He was on the road to the cross and the days leading up to His crucifixion, He could have given up at any point. After all, He was innocent! He didn't deserve one bit of the punishment he endured on our behalf. But He did it anyway. He saw that fighting the good fight and finishing the race was worth it and did whatever it took to get there. He never gave up.

Whatever you are facing today, please know that Jesus is with you. He wants to help you. He is your strength when you are weak. He gives you peace that surpasses anything you can imagine. Your life circumstances are never too big for God. He is all you need to be able to stay wherever He has called you no matter how dark it feels. He is your light that guides you!

We have written our newest study *The Wise Woman Stays* for this purpose. Whatever the area is in your life that God has asked you to be faithful and obedient, *listen and follow Him.* He is the Shepherd of your heart and knows exactly what you need. As you read the words of these pages and ponder the idea of "staying," ask God to reveal Himself to you and shed light on where you need to stay and be faithful. Jesus delights in your steadfastness!

Numbers 6:24-26 says, "May the Lord bless you and keep you; The Lord make His face shine upon you, And be gracious to you; The Lord lift up His countenance upon you, And give you peace."

With Love,
Krystle and The Help Club for Moms Team

The Wise Woman Stays

Summer of Staying

~ Week One ~

Hello Friends!

This is it! The sun has returned, and the glorious days of summer are awakening before us! Such a prospect of hope these days carry! Sister, God is calling you to stay faithful to His purpose for you as you fill each crevice of this season with the love of Jesus! However, if you are anything like me, you may quickly find your patience running thin and your feet inching ever closer to the life door marked "exit." How can we remain faithful to that first summer calling, especially when the natural path our lives take is much less rosy?

I'll tell you, the way God has called me to stay faithful is to simply take one small step forward at a time—one morning at a time in His Word, one smile of gentleness toward a disobedient child, one loving thought toward my husband, one prayer instead of a sharp word, one continual reach out to Jesus instead of withdrawing into myself—one step, every minute, every day, toward the woman God is calling me to be.

When you stay near the Lord, He will guide you, strengthen you, and infuse your summer with the peace and joy you so desire. God's Word is a lamp to our feet and a light to our path (Psalm 119:105). He will shine that warm light on your path this summer, enabling you to take one small step at a time toward becoming the woman, wife, and mother He is creating you to be. And if you get off course, just turn around and take one small step back toward your Savior and living a life radiating with His love. Stay right where the Lord wants you to be this summer! His grace is sufficient for you, my friend! And this long, lovely summer doesn't have to be perfect to be beautiful. It simply needs to be one small step at a time in the direction of faithfulness.

Love and Blessings,
Tara Davis and the Help Club for Moms Team

> *The steadfast love of the Lord never ceases;*
> *his mercies never come to an end;*
> *they are new every morning;*
> *great is your faithfulness.*
>
> *~ Lamentations 3:22-23 (ESV)*

By: Leslie Leonard

"Be kind to one another, tenderhearted, forgiving one another, as God in Christ forgave you." ~ Ephesians 4:32 (ESV)

The Wise Woman Builds Her Spirit:

- Download a voice recording app on your phone to help you get ready to memorize Scripture from the studies. If you do not have a smartphone, purchase an inexpensive voice recording device. As we go through the studies record any verses that you'd like to memorize.

- Get a pad of spiral bound index cards and write 1 Peter 5:7-10 in it. Keep it at your kitchen sink so that you will see it often and commit it to memory.

The Wise Woman Loves Her Husband:

- Take a walk with your husband this week. Get outside and enjoy the fresh air together. Take the time to reconnect and talk with one another.

- Pray for your husband while he drives to work this week. Pray that he will have wisdom, patience, and grace with those he comes into contact with during his time out of the home.

The Wise Woman Loves Her Children:

- Head to your local library this week and check out some new books to read together as a family. While you are there, don't forget to sign up for the Summer Reading Program if your local library hosts one.

- Help your children memorize Ephesians 4:32. Write it on your chalkboard or bathroom mirror. Use this verse to help your children understand the importance of choosing to be kind, even when it's a hard choice.

The Wise Woman Cares For Her Home:

- Know what is for dinner by 9:00 a.m. every day this week:

  Monday:_____ Tuesday:_____ Wednesday:_____

  Thursday:_____ Friday:_____

- Exercise self-control with your family budget this week. Do not overspend or ignore your preset financial boundaries. If you do not have a family budget, take this week to create one prayerfully with your spouse.

> His master replied, 'Well done, good and faithful servant! You have been faithful with a few things; I will put you in charge of many things. Come and share your master's happiness!'
> ~ Matthew 25:23

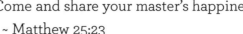

Six Little Words

By: Deb Weakly

"Well done, good and faithful servant" (Matthew 25:23a). These six little words make up the declaration every believer in Jesus Christ longs to hear when finished with life on this earth. I can't even imagine how glorious it will be to awaken someday in heaven and hear the voice of our Savior tenderly speaking the precious words, "Well done, good and faithful servant."

How about you, mama? Do you ever think about the end of your life and how you want to finish? A good and faithful life happens one day at a time, one moment at a time while holding the hand of Jesus and trusting Him to help us live and love well.

As mamas, even as we walk with Jesus, our calling to these virtues can still feel challenging. Sometimes our lives get so hard and our circumstances make us want to throw in the towel or even give up on the lives God has called us to live. We may have difficulty in our marriages and feel like they are never going to get any better. Perhaps the weariness of the day-in-day-out life with a difficult child makes us want to run away and hide or check out altogether. Or worst of all, we may feel far away and distant from God Himself and be too "busy" to even spend time with Him.

Oh sweet mama, life does get hard, but I can tell you from experience that if we will listen carefully each moment for the voice of our sweet Jesus, we will hear Him beckoning us: *Hang in there, don't give up, live each day with Me.* He is our faithful Shepherd, the one who, "...tends his flock like a shepherd: He gathers the lambs in his arms and carries them close to his heart; he gently leads those that have young" (Isaiah 40:11).

Don't give up, dear one. Jesus is right there with you. Listen for His voice today. Take the words of Winston Churchill to heart, "Never, ever, ever, ever, ever, ever, ever, give up. Never give up. Never give up. Never give up." I think that about sums it up!

Go Deeper:
• Prayerfully ask the Lord to tell you if there are any areas of your life in which you are disengaged or want to quit. Ask God to help you stay faithful, no matter what!

What's Next?

The book you are holding in your hands is a tool to help you live your life well and stay faithful to the ones the Lord has called you to love. The book is titled *The Wise Woman Stays* because it is our heart's desire to encourage you as a mom to stay engaged and involved in your life, even when it's tough.

Each day, as you read through this book, ask the Holy Spirit to speak to your heart and help you obey what He tells you. Be sure to write what you feel Him saying to you in a journal or spiral notebook. This is such an important step in learning what it means to live your life well.

I love how the authors of the study *Experiencing God* put it:

> When the God of the universe tells you something, it's important enough to write down. When God speaks to you in your quiet times with Him, immediately record what He says, before you forget. Then add your prayer response.

This advice has helped me learn how to hear the voice of God in a practical way. I pray it helps you too!

journal

_____

_____

_____

_____

_____

_____

_____

_____

_____

_____

_____

_____

_____

_____

_____

_____

_____

_____

_____

_____

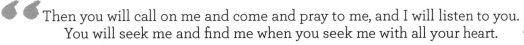

> "Then you will call on me and come and pray to me, and I will listen to you. You will seek me and find me when you seek me with all your heart.
>
> ~ Jeremiah 29:12-13

Linger Longer in the Lord's Embrace

By: Rachel Jones

Being a mom is hard. It is a long road lined with tireless nights, thankless days, sad moments, and many hopeless thoughts. Often, you just want a nice person to come take your kids away and give you a full day of peace.

Mama, I am writing today to tell you that you are *not* alone! We all feel this way and it is normal. Raising kids is exhausting, but it is *the* most important work. However, a good mama cannot pour into her kids from an empty well. Every mother needs to take time for herself to be with God and soak in His presence. He invites us in James 4:8 to do just that, "Draw near to God and He will draw near to you."

The ironic part about being a mom is that we are often our own worst enemies. We desperately need Jesus to help us parent well, but we are so busy and focused on our kids that we push Him aside and occasionally offer Him a few pathetic crumbs of affection. What we need to do is constantly linger near Jesus and cuddle up to Him.

Staying in His embrace reveals truths about our thoughts and helps us be able to detect Satan's lies...those lies that creep into our minds and say, b*eing a mom is too hard* or *I can't do this anymore.* We are instructed in Psalm 46:10 to "be still, and know that I am God." The wording "be still" literally means to cease from striving. It means you are allowed to let go and relax, to turn down the volume of the world (or your kids!), and to listen to the quiet whisper of God.

Our precious children all deserve a mom who answers with a smile, gives hugs freely, and cooks meals gladly. Psalm 27:8 is one of my favorite, simple verses. The ending, "Your face Lord, I will seek," is a gentle reminder to focus on Him. Do not look at anything but His face and His reassuring promises this summer! We all need to be more attentive this summer, to the Lord and to our children. Let's strive to gain our joy, encouragement, and purpose from the correct source—Jesus.

Go Deeper:
• As you think about today's study, pray and ask God to come nearer to you than ever before. Read over all the verses I mentioned above and meditate on them.

What's Next?
After the kids go to bed one night this week, take some alone time. Let your husband know so he doesn't think you are ignoring him.

You could sit on your deck or patio with a blanket and look at the stars, thinking, listening, and praying as you do. You could take a bubble bath with the lights turned off and only a candle lit or listen to some light worship music and think, listen, and pray.

I pray this time is special and relaxing. But mostly, I pray the Lord meets you and reveals some new truths to you!

journal

> " Young people, it's wonderful to be young! Enjoy every minute of it.
> Do everything you want to do; take it all in. But remember
> that you must give an account to God for everything you do. "
>
> ~ Ecclesiastes 11:9 (NLT)

Make the Most of Your Summer

By: Heather Doolittle

Summer is the perfect time to teach your children about God's love and the gifts He has given all of us: nature, art, entertainment, laughter, family, and friends! "Every good and perfect gift is from above" (James 1:17), and so we should take the time to enjoy the good gifts God has given us and teach our children to recognize them as such. Here are some tips for making the most of your summer:

- **Instill a love of learning**

  Learning can be fun! Instilling a love of learning in your children is one of the most important gifts you can give them. Ask your kids what interests them and find a variety of resources for them to explore, such as library books, documentaries, toys, puzzles, and audiobooks. Children don't need to be taught everything; they will often be more excited about the knowledge they obtain for themselves. Leonardo da Vinci is one of the greatest intellectuals in history. Not only was he a gifted artist, but his work as a scientist and inventor was far ahead of his time. He learned the foundations of all of these skills by carefully observing nature and filling his journals with detailed notes and sketches about what he saw. Like da Vinci, a child who loves to learn will have the whole world as a classroom. Observing the details of a butterfly's wings at the park, reading the signs about animals at the zoo, and experimenting by making clay pots from backyard mud are just a few memorable, fun, and educational experiences.

- **Get your hands dirty**

  Participate with your kids. I didn't realize how seldom I actually shared experiences with my kids until we moved a few years ago. They generally played with their friends while I chatted with the moms. With our friends out of the picture, my kids wanted me to do things like swim with them and go down the water slide instead of sitting poolside, and it was a great bonding experience for all of us. Now that we have settled in and made friends, my children would rather play with other kids than their mom, and I am happy to have some grown-up time. However, we still schedule outings and play times just for us, and we all look forward to it.

- **Explore your city**

  Another great habit we established during our move was exploring our surroundings by trying out new parks and libraries, going to museums and cultural events, spending time in different neighborhoods, and learning the history of our city. I married an East-Coaster whose love of the mountains brought him to Colorado, so we have always spent weekends hiking and checking out different parts of the state. But I lived in Colorado Springs for ten years, and there were many parts of town I never visited and events I never got around to attending. I went to my favorite places and stayed within my comfort zone, but when I moved, I had no comfort zone. Even now, I realize that I have fallen into the same rut in my new home, so I plan to go somewhere new every week (even if it's just trying out a different Wal-Mart).

Corinthians 10:31 tells us, "So whether you eat or drink or whatever you do, do it all for the glory of God." Friends, I hope you have a fantastic summer, enjoying the warm weather and your family. Do it all for the glory of God and reap the benefits of a joyful family!

Go Deeper:

- Do you take the time to interact with your kids, play with them, and experience life together? How can you make it a priority to do this more?

- What are some new experiences you think your kids might enjoy?

- What are the activities they love that you never seem to find time to do?

What's Next?

Incorporate the categories above as well as anything that is important to you into your calendar. If I don't make a goal to play with my kids or go somewhere new on a set day each week, I will never do it. You can be flexible; rearrange your plans if something else comes up. Just make sure you're rescheduling these important items so they don't fall by the wayside. We are moms, and we are all busy. It takes intentionality to avoid falling into a rut and living under the tyranny of the urgent.

Write down the verses in this study, and tell your kids that God loves them and has given them so many gifts. He wants us to make the most of our time and enjoy this gift of life!

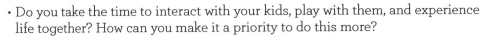

_____

_____

_____

_____

_____

_____

_____

_____

_____

_____

_____

_____

> " Jesus left there and went along the sea of Galilee. Then he went up on the mountainside and sat down. Great crowds came to him, bringing the lame, the blind, the crippled, the mute, and many others, and laid them at his feet; and he healed them... Jesus called his disciples to him and said, 'I have compassion for these people...' "
>
> ~ Matthew 15:29-32

Children Are the Most Important Work

By: Susan Proctor

C.S. Lewis said, "Children are not a distraction from more important work. They are the most important work." Recently, I have been extremely convicted about how I treat my eight children: I sometimes treat them as a distraction rather than important work. I set out my agenda each day, and my focus and ability to feel good about myself sometimes rests on how many things I can check off that list. I utilize the summer months to reorganize and deep clean our home. Yet, some days I get bombarded by curious children, emotional teenagers, and teething babies. I treat my most prized possessions as a distraction when they are the core of my "job."

Jesus never treated anyone like a distraction. In Matthew 15, Jesus had compassion on the hungry crowds and fed them. When He would escape to the mountains, the crowd would follow Him and He would heal "the lame, the blind, the deformed, those unable to speak and many others" (Matthew 15:30). The result was that they would give praise and glory to God. Jesus utilized every moment.

I want my children to give praise and glory to God because I was able to speak life. When my boys have an argument and need me to help work it out, I need to see it as an opportunity to learn the gift of conflict resolution. When I am in the middle of sorting out toy bins, I need to take the time and answer my daughter's curious questions. I need to see the valuable lesson of teaching self-control to my sweet three-year-old in the middle of the grocery store. When I sit down to read my Bible and the baby wakes up too early, I need to be patient and teach the importance of reading God's Word even if it is in small increments.

This summer, let all of us strive to use everyday situations as a way to teach, to love, to nurture, to honor, and to be. Oh Lord, helps us remember that our precious ones are our greater work. Help us remember that the days are long, but the years are oh, so short.

Go Deeper:

- Read Matthew 15. Note when Jesus withdraws from the crowd and His reaction or response.
- Write out some ways you can respond when you feel like you are being distracted by a child.

What's Next?

Five years ago, my children and I began a journey to add a little fun to every summer day. We called it "No Bummer Summer." Every day, I would come up with one fun thing we could do as a family. For example, we would have water balloon fights, car races, science experiments, game days, park days, homemade ice cream parties, and so many other things. Make a list of fun things to do this summer and pick one to do each day. Your family will love it, and your relationships will flourish.

journal

Food for the Soul

I've often said food is my love language. I enjoy and appreciate all kinds of food, and I also love to cook for others. Whether it is a simple recipe or something I spend all day cooking, I love sharing my joy of food. There is something special about how food can recall notable memories from childhood or important times in our lives. It brings people together for many occasions— holidays, sports, girls' nights, parties, birthdays, etc. Food can even bring people comfort during illnesses or difficult times in their lives. Food plays a major role in distinguishing cultures and bringing them right into our homes for us to experience.

If we have a little extra time on the weekend, a favorite special breakfast that my family loves is our version of egg soufflés. These are little muffin cups of buttery pastry with a creamy, cheesy egg filling. My daughter is gluten-free, and one of the great things about this recipe is that you can easily make it gluten-free. You can also make these any flavor you want by incorporating any flavor additions to the egg base. The possibilities are endless. We make at least two different flavors at a time for variety, and everyone can have some made with their favorite flavor. These little gems reheat well in the oven, so don't be afraid of making too many! We hope you enjoy them as much as we do. They are not as hard to make as you may think, so try them!

EGG SOUFFLÉS WITH GLUTEN-FREE OPTION

By: Brandi Carson

Ingredients:

2 tablespoons butter

2 tablespoons flour, white all-purpose or gluten-free sweet white rice flour

1-1 ½ cup half-and-half

6 eggs, beaten

½ to ¾ cup cheese of your choice. The stronger the cheese, the less you need.

½-¾ cup cheese (additional) to sprinkle on top

1-1 ½ cup filling flavors: bacon, sun-dried tomatoes, veggies of your choice, a variety of cheeses, ham, spinach or kale, caramelized onions, breakfast meats, or whatever your heart desires. Be creative!

2 packages of pre-made crescent rolls or gluten-free pie crust

Directions:

1. In a large saucepan, melt butter over medium heat.

2. Whisk in white flour or gluten-free flour until well-mixed. If making the gluten-free option, make sure to use sweet rice flour. It works well as a thickener, which not all gluten-free flours are good for.

3. Add 1 cup of half-and-half and cook on medium heat until thickened, whisking frequently. Do not let boil. If it seems really thick like paste, add an extra ½ cup of half and half. Cook until it reaches consistency of white gravy. Remove from heat.

EGG SOUFFLÉS

Directions (continued):

4. Whisk in cheese(s) of choice. Be generous! When cheese is melted, whisk in eggs one at a time, making sure eggs are thoroughly incorporated each time you add an additional egg.

5. At this point, mix in any fillings desired. If you want to try two different flavors of soufflé, divide the egg mixture into separate bowls and add different fillings to each bowl. You may also want to reserve some of the fillings to sprinkle on top of the soufflé, like cheese or bacon, etc.

6. Preheat oven to 375 degrees.

7. Spray muffin pans with baking spray, making sure to spray the top of the muffin pan as well as the interior of each muffin cup generously. Fill each muffin cup with either ¼-⅓" thick gluten-free pie crust or a triangle of crescent roll dough. You want the dough to completely fill each muffin cup and overflow a bit, overlapping the top of the pan. For the crescent rolls, you will have to cut the triangle dough in half and press it back together in the shape of a square to fit in the muffin cup. The gluten-free pie crust can get crumbly, press it into the pan until you get the desired thickness.

8. When muffin cups are all covered with dough, fill each cup ¾ full of egg soufflé batter. Sprinkle top with any additional cheese or desired toppings.

9. Bake for 15 to 20 minutes or until it no longer jiggles and center is cooked through. Use a knife or toothpick to check. The soufflés will rise a lot during baking and get really puffy, but once out of the oven and cooled slightly, they will collapse a little.

10. Let cool for a few minutes before serving. You may need to run a butter knife along the edges and underneath the crust to remove the soufflés from the pan.

Summer of Staying

~ Week Two ~

I'm done! I can't take this anymore! This is too much for me!

Dearest Mama,

Do you ever feel like saying these words? We all do! Life is hard, and messy. We are sinful mamas who live in houses with sinful little (and big) people who can say and do things that make us want to give up and throw in the towel. Day after day, we try to be good wives and mothers, and then something happens to make us feel like we want to run and hide, to just get away from it all.

The Bible says we have an enemy who "prowls around like a roaring lion looking for someone to devour" (1 Peter 5:8). Satan opposes the people of God. He hates Christian families, so he will try to do all he can to try to destroy yours. Often he will try to coerce you into giving up on your marriage, a child, and even yourself.

The amazing news is that the Bible also says that we have a Savior who overcame the devil and, as Christ-followers, His Holy Spirit lives inside each of us and helps us live our lives with power and victory!

> I pray that the eyes of your heart may be enlightened in order that you may know the hope to which he has called you, the riches of his glorious inheritance in his holy people, and his incomparably **great power** for us who believe. That **power** is the same as the mighty strength he exerted when he raised Christ from the dead and seated him at his right hand in the heavenly realms. (Ephesians 1:18-20)

Friend, you have the power of the Holy Spirit living inside of you! This power is so great that we have to pray for the eyes of our hearts to be enlightened in order to even understand this truth! My challenge for you today is to pray and ask God to help you understand this power you have to help you keep going, even when you feel like giving up. I am praying for you today.

With love,
Deb Weakly and the Help Club for Moms Team

> **"** *We must learn to live on the heavenly side and look at things from above. To contemplate all things as God sees them, as Christ beholds them, overcomes sin, defies Satan, dissolves perplexities, lifts us above trials, separates us from the world and conquers fear of death.* **"**
>
> ~ A.B. Simpson

Mom Tips

By: Leslie Leonard

"For God gave us a spirit not of fear but of power and love and self-control." ~ 2 Timothy 1:7 (ESV)

The Wise Woman Builds Her Spirit:

- Connect with your prayer partner this week. Plan to pray together for 10 minutes. If you need to, schedule a social call at the beginning of your prayer time so you can focus during your call.

- Summer can get hectic and overwhelming very quickly. Take 10 minutes every evening to just sit in the quiet and breathe. Close your eyes, turn off any distractions, and clear your mind. Listen to your breathing and allow yourself to just be.

The Wise Woman Loves Her Husband:

- Arrange a "Date Night In" for the two of you this week. Plan an activity that both of you really enjoy or choose something that you have both been wanting to try out (like a new board game or cooking technique). Wait until the kids are in bed and spend some quality time together that does not involve the television.

- Pray for your husband this week. Pray that his spiritual gifts will be used in all aspects of his life (work, home, church, and leisure). You can pray 1 Corinthians 12:4 specifically.

The Wise Woman Loves Her Children:

- Create a Summer Bucket List with your children. Have each child participate and make a poster to hang in your kitchen. Use stickers or a marker to check off the list when you complete an item.

- Learn a new Praise and Worship song as a family. Bonus if someone plays a musical instrument and can accompany along with the singing.

The Wise Woman Cares For Her Home:

- Clean off the top of your refrigerator this week. Clear off the clutter and wipe down the entire space.

- Dust all of the baseboards and blinds/window treatments in your home this week. Pick a room a day and the task will be completed easily by the end of the week.

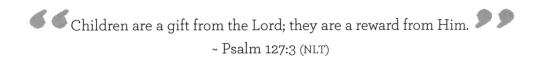

" Children are a gift from the Lord; they are a reward from Him. **"**

~ Psalm 127:3 (NLT)

Draw Your Children Close This Summer

By: Tara Davis

It is finally summer! But instead of simply viewing this time as a break, choose to see it as an opportunity to purposefully pour the love of Christ into the hearts of your children! This is the season to strengthen your relationship with your children and point them again to their Savior!

Just as our Good Shepherd gathers us close to His heart, He is calling you to draw your little lambs close to yours (Isaiah 40:11). As you intentionally tie heartstrings of love with your children, you will have a more effective impact on their lives and their walks with Jesus. Be faithful to the work of motherhood, my friend. You are making an impact on eternity!

Here are some ideas to help make this summer the most precious, influential time with your children:

- **Morning Time** – While your children are eating breakfast, you have a perfectly captive audience! Read a short devotion or Proverb and discuss, pray together, and recite a Bible verse. Choose a hymn for the summer and sing it every day. This is a great way to begin the day—with hearts focused on Jesus!

- **Snuggle Parties** – Take time to cuddle your children (or even just sit together)! Lay blankets outside at night and gather close while looking at stars, or grab a big stack of books and pile in bed together to read aloud. You could also sit with your children on the couch and talk about anything they want to discuss! Just be together!

- **Creation Glasses** – God has given us eyes to see His fingerprints all around us! Notice God's wonder in creation with your children! Start a nature box or table to collect and learn about God's world. Point out the majesty of our Creator to your children!

- **Play Time** – Take a few minutes out of your day to do something that your kids enjoy. On days when tension and frustration run high, do something physical together to alleviate some of the stress.

- **Thankful Contests** – Keep a family list of things you can thank God for. Always be on the lookout for small blessings and write them down!

- **Prayer Stops** – Be intentional about praying for your children this summer! Pray out loud over them, blessing their lives and thanking God for specific qualities they exhibit. Make note of one or two verses you can pray for each of your children this summer.

Go Deeper:

- The Lord so very tenderly draws His children to a right standing with Him. Hosea 11:4 declares, "I drew them with gentle cords, with bands of love, and I was to them as those who take the yoke from their neck. I stooped and fed them" (NKJV). Take a few minutes to consider the Lord's love for you! Friends, let's be ambassadors of Christ's love in our homes as we apply this verse to our relationships with our children.

What's Next?

Five years ago, my children and I began a journey to add a little fun to every summer day. We called it "No Bummer Summer." Every day, I would come up with one fun thing we could do as a family. For example, we would have water balloon fights, car races, science experiments, game days, park days, homemade ice cream parties, and so many other things. Make a list of fun things to do this summer and pick one to do each day. Your family will love it, and your relationships will flourish.

journal

_____

_____

_____

_____

_____

_____

_____

_____

_____

_____

_____

_____

_____

_____

_____

_____

_____

_____

_____

_____

_____

_____

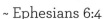

> Do not exasperate your children; instead,
> bring them up in the training and instruction of the Lord.
>
> ~ Ephesians 6:4

Created for True Love

By: Mari Jo Mast

When my children were younger, I struggled to keep my head above water. They required so much of my time and attention and were naughty (like, a lot). It seemed to escalate every time we were with friends or in public, and I felt overwhelmed when they misbehaved. Out of desperation and pride, I constantly tried to stop and control the bad behavior. I wanted "microwave kids"—to push a button and make them instantly holy. I was weary and longed for quick results.

A well-meaning person told me to discipline my children *every* time they disobeyed, talked back, or displayed a wrong attitude. It was explained that if I didn't punish every single time, it would allow rebellion to run rampant in our home (rebellion is like witchcraft, you know). We had a handful of kids at the time, so you can imagine how impossible this was. But I believed her and wanted to be a "good" mom so I diligently tried to follow her advice.

It grieves my heart as I remember: I became a policeman in my own home. I "arrested" the kids all day long, keeping track of their "crimes." I thought I could somehow force them into submission.

However, our children can't be made instantly holy. They can't even be "good" by God's standard until the Holy Spirit comes to live inside of them. What they need is for us to show them "the Way."

My own methods could never create a true heart change. What I was focusing on only strengthened their sin! When you concentrate on punishing and correcting bad behavior all the time, that's what happens. What if God always watched and punished us immediately for every wrong thing we did? I'm pretty sure most of us would no longer be alive!

Yes, what my children really needed was more of Jesus—to be discipled in His Truth, with words of *life* and blessing spoken over them. I needed godly vision to see, to minister genuine kindness and loving instruction. They needed love—a love that showed pure enjoyment in our relationship, one that cherished and nurtured their tender hearts just as Jesus daily exemplified to me. I needed to live a life of servanthood and be an example of patience, even in the middle of disobedience. They needed a quiet confidence of their right standing with me—that they will always be loved, no matter how badly they behave. They needed me to pull them out of their sin, and to help lead them to the one who bore all of their sins.

Parenting like Jesus won't bring "instant" holiness. Instead, it takes lots and lots of time and commitment. It takes repentance and the Holy Spirit.

Sweet, sweet mama, be careful who you listen to. When we become overwhelmed and desperate, we do crazy things we regret later. Our children are precious, created with dignity and made in the image of God—just like we are. We will give an account someday of how we steward the ones He entrusts to us.

Below are a few practical keys listed that help me to this day. I hope they will encourage you too in your mothering journey! They are simple yet profound and all of it comes from God's Word. His wisdom is far greater than ours and so practical. Truly His ways are genius and life-changing!

- **Relax:** Make an allowance for your kid's faults because you love them (Ephesians 4:2). They *are* going to mess up, and it's ok. Jesus already knows, and that's why He came! Lead them to the one who gives them the power to overcome sin.

- **Be Humble**: Don't parent out of pride. If your kid misbehaves in public or acts up around your friend's kids, smile and tell them, "So sorry, we're trying to work on this right now." Admit it when your kids are wrong, but don't shame them.

- **Be Gentle**: Proverbs 15:1 (NKJV) says, "A soft answer turns away wrath, but a harsh word stirs up anger." Try not to raise your voice, and instead try to speak gently. This totally works!

- **Be Patient**: James 1:19 (NLT) says, "You must all be quick to listen, slow to speak, and slow to get angry." Hear with your heart, not your head, and filter, filter, filter with love.

- **Be Led By The Holy Spirit**: Galatians 5:18 (NKJV) says, "But if you are led by the Spirit, you are not under the Law." Wow, think about this! In the middle of a conflict, pause for a while and ask God what He thinks. Carefully listen and then obey. The Spirit gives *life*, but the law strengthens sin.

- **Choose to live in peace**: (Ephesians 4:3b). Don't be worried or troubled—instead, trust God with your kids. Let the Shalom of God reign in your heart!

Go Deeper:

- What has motherhood looked like for you? Who are you listening to? Are you struggling to see your child/children as a gift from God's hand because of bad behavior? God wants to help you be a better mom. With His help, how can you improve?

What's Next?

Over the next five weeks, try to memorize these five passages of Scripture. They will help ground you as a mom. Write them down on sticky notes and place them on your bathroom mirror, in your car, or even on a marker board. Place them where you will see them often.

- Ephesians 4:2   • Proverbs 15:1   • James 1:19   • Galatians 5:17-18   • Ephesians 4:3

journal

_____

_____

_____

_____

_____

_____

_____

_____

> " He who gathers during summer and takes advantage
> of his opportunities is a son who acts wisely. "
>
> ~ Proverbs 10:5

The Opportunity of Summer: Renewing Your Child's Mind & Family Relationships

By: Tara Fox

The Bible tells us, "Do not conform to the pattern of this world but be transformed by the renewing of your mind. Then you will be able to test and approve what God's will is—his good, pleasing and perfect will" (Romans 12:2). With school completed for the year and schedules more relaxed, summer is the perfect opportunity for your children to renew their minds and their family relationships through spending time in God's Word. In our family, we like to do our devotions right after breakfast to ensure this important time doesn't get pushed aside.

Mama, one of the best uses of your time is to teach your children about God. Take advantage of the summer to teach your children what you are learning from the Lord. Mull over the Bible as God leads you. Read excellent, godly books and devotions. Linger in worship and dance together. When the Lord is leading, you will be so amazed at how He ties your devotion time with your children together. When we are finished with our family devotion time in the morning, I find that it is a beautiful transition to send my children away to spend their own time with the Lord.

While your children spend alone time with the Lord, give them freedom to journal, color, read, listen to worship, dance, or just be quiet and listen. The only thing I require is that they are alone with God. Keep it as short as they need. Have supplies available that match their interests. You will know when they are ready for this time. If you have little ones, they can sit right next to you as you model. It's so fun to watch your children's relationships with God blossom as they realize they too can spend time with Him.

After a special summer focusing on God and retreating a bit from the world, I believe your children will desire to continue this precious time with their Heavenly Father into the next season.

Summer is also a unique time for children to slow down from other commitments and just be together. If we are faithful to initiate this needed time, it can bring a lot of life to our homes.

It is important to keep ongoing discussions about their relationships with their siblings. They need our help to see the big picture. We can ask questions like, "What do you want your relationship with your siblings to be like in five, ten, or thirty years from now?" Discuss how their treatment of each other now will affect the outcome of their relationships in the future. We can show our children that their siblings are their built-in best friends. This mostly happens as a result of spending more time together than with other friends outside the home.

When school is out and children are less scheduled, they often fight and argue more. No matter the season, if my children are having a hard time with each other, I know they may need alone time

Week Two ~ Day Three

with my husband or me to affirm and build them up personally, or they may need one-on-one time with their siblings to bond and strengthen their relationships with each other. We have three children in our family, so sometimes one child is left out. My oldest and youngest are further apart and need encouragement to spend time together.

It is helpful for our children to look within themselves instead of blaming others. Discuss together what little changes they can make that will make a big difference in their relationships with their siblings. Talk about having humility, not being easily offended, forgiving quickly, helping each other, not teasing, believing the best, initiating play, and desiring to be together. Help them to understand that if they can handle conflict well inside their home, they will be able to master it with others outside their home. God intends for our home to be a safe place in which we can practice with those who love us.

I know God is going to fill you and your family with His love and goodness as you seek Him. May this be a summer to remember!

Go Deeper:

- Are your children having difficulty keeping peace with each other? It is helpful to pray about it and observe their interactions to get to the heart issues. Is God impressing on your heart any particular cause, such as lack of attention, insecurity, jealousy, or not feeling loved? If we can get to the root, we can help our children overcome these problems that are affecting them and the family as a whole.

- Are you getting your daily time in with the Lord? If not, this is never something we should feel guilty about but instead should ask God to give us the time to spend with Him. He's not mad at you when it doesn't happen, He just misses you and looks forward to the next time you will have together!

What's Next?

Make a devotion basket for your children. Some things you could include are a Bible, Scripture coloring book, colored pencils, Scripture memory cards, a worship CD, and a journal.

journal

_____

_____

_____

_____

_____

_____

_____

_____

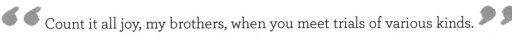

> **"** Count it all joy, my brothers, when you meet trials of various kinds. **"**
>
> ~ James 1:2 (ESV)

Choosing Joy

By: Leslie Leonard

Do you ever hear clichés that make you cringe every time you hear them leave someone's lips? Some of those phrases for me are "Bless her heart," or "She is such a sweet spirit." There is one, in particular, that seems to make my blood pressure rise the most: "What doesn't kill you makes you stronger." Really? My only two choices are the current trial I am facing in my life or *death*? I choose door number three instead. This phrase is wrong. We, as believers in Jesus Christ, do not find our joy and strength through the trials or events in our lives. We find our joy and strength through the redemptive power of Jesus Christ. Psalm 73:26 tells us, "My flesh and my heart may fail, but God is the strength of my heart and my portion forever."

I want to take you on my personal journey over the last 22 months. I have walked in the darkest season I have known as a believer. My life is challenging in several different areas: struggles with my oldest daughter, my health, and lack of close friendships. Perhaps your life is challenging too. I have never been in a place of such severe loneliness and frustration before in all of my days.

More often than I care to admit, I have asked Jesus to just end it all, to find a way to quickly take me from this earth so I would no longer have to endure the pain and anxiety of life. Some days, I literally hate getting up in the mornings because of the great unknown that is ahead of me. Coffee is my constant companion because sleep does not come at night. I move through life in a fog, a shadow of my former self. I know that I am not living the joy-filled life that I was created by God to live.

Beloved, we must choose joy. "We are destroying speculations and every lofty thing raised up against the knowledge of God, and we are taking every thought captive to the obedience of Christ" (2 Corinthians 10:5 NASB). Give your thoughts to Jesus and ask Him to help to help you choose joy. We are not expected to anything on our own. In fact, John 15:5 says, "Apart from me you can do nothing."

With the help of Jesus Christ, we can choose to be joyful even if we are sad, lonely, or angry. True, lasting joy is the direct result of trusting God one day at a time and keeping in step with the Holy Spirit. When we choose to trust God fully with our lives, we can experience joy.

An eye-opening moment came for me recently. My oldest daughter stood on the edge of the swimming pool, adjusted her bright blue and green swimsuit and dove right into the deep end. No hesitation or fear, she just knew she could complete the task. I realized at that moment that I am doing her a disservice when I do not see her through the eyes of Jesus. You see, I was unsure of my daughter's ability, but she had complete faith. In the same way, Jesus is always ready to love us, no matter what broken tools we carry around in our toolbox.

God's heart for His daughters is that we walk in our identity in Jesus, not in a fleshy estimation of ourselves. Joy comes from seeing with eyes of the Spirit. The enemy cannot maintain a stronghold on our hearts and minds if we choose to align them with the Lord Most High. I know that when I swap a negative thought or emotion with a positive one, actively choosing joy, I push the enemy aside and prove to him (and myself) that he has no power over me. Exchanging thoughts is a powerful tool that allows us to make an immediate change in our lives.

Week Two ~ Day Four

So, what have I learned during this dark and stormy season of my life? Prayer is comforting and necessary, and more than leaning on anyone else, lean on Jesus. Let Him provide you with the comfort and safe place that you so desperately seek. Proverbs 56:8 reminds us that He is listening even when we cannot find the words to speak out loud. Friends, He hears you, He loves you, and He is *always* walking by your side. Satan will push you to believe that you are walking through life alone, so you must guard your hearts (Proverbs 4:23). When you are facing sadness or hardship, always seek Jesus first in prayer.

I would like to be able to tell you that I am a completely changed woman. I will tell you that I am a work in progress. I trust God to guide me in my journey to be the best mother and wife because He placed me on this path with my husband and gave me two awe-inspiring children. My life *is* worth getting out of bed for in the morning! I choose joy!

Go Deeper:

· Write the following verses on notecards or in your journal. Please try to memorize these verses. They are powerful verses about trusting the Lord in all circumstances.

· Psalm 13:5   · 1 Thessalonians 5:16-18   · James 1:2-4   · Nehemiah 8:10b

· In your journal, define the words *content* and *satisfied* in your own words. Be specific and detailed in your answer.

What's Next?

Have you ever started a gratitude or blessing journal? It's a very simple way to focus on all the good that God has done in your life. It is a wonderful source of joy. You can go back and reflect on all God has done in your life!

Journal

_____

_____

_____

_____

_____

_____

_____

_____

_____

_____

_____

_____

10 Scriptures to pray for your Summer!

1. You will keep in perfect peace those whose minds are steadfast, because they trust in you. **Isaiah 26:3**

2. Be completely humble and gentle; be patient, bearing with one another in love. **Ephesians 4:2**

3. Consider it pure joy, my brothers, and sisters, whenever you face trials of many kinds. **James 1:2**

4. Let us not become weary in doing good, for at the proper time we will reap a harvest if we do not give up. **Galatians 6:9**

5. Therefore do not worry about tomorrow, for tomorrow will worry about itself. Each day has enough trouble of its own. **Matthew 6:34**

6. Great is his faithfulness; his mercies begin afresh each morning. **Lamentations 3:23**

7. Finally, brothers and sisters, whatever is true, whatever is noble, whatever is right, whatever is pure, whatever is lovely, whatever is admirable—if anything is excellent or praiseworthy—think about such things. **Philippians 4:8**

8. Rejoice always, pray without ceasing, give thanks in all circumstances; for this is the will of God in Christ Jesus for you. **1 Thessalonians 5:16-18**

9. He settles the childless woman in her home as a happy mother of children. Praise the Lord. **Psalm 113:9**

10. Behold, how good and pleasant it is when brothers dwell in unity! **Psalm 133:1 (ESV)**

Week Two

_____

_____

_____

_____

_____

_____

_____

_____

_____

_____

_____

_____

_____

_____

_____

_____

_____

_____

_____

_____

_____

_____

_____

_____

_____

_____

_____

_____

Summer of Staying

~ Week Three ~

My Dear Sister,

The non-stop, crazy, calendar-filled last days of school have ended, but then comes the wind down—sorting through all the papers from the school year, finalizing vacation plans and summer camps, and finding that half-eaten sandwich at the very bottom of the backpack. When that's all done, you grab a refreshing drink, sit down to relax, and then read about...Back to School sales?! Where did the summer go?

Yes, this is an exaggeration, but do you sometimes feel like even though you're in the middle of summer, you can't relax? Are you tired of trying to remember which child goes to which camp or if you have enough sleeping bags or what happened to all the sunblock?!

James 4:14 says, "Why, you do not even know what will happen tomorrow. What is your life? You are a mist that appears for a little while and then vanishes." The context of this verse relates to boasting and spending time doing business without submitting to God. How does this relate to our job of mothering?

You, dear mama, are not a "cog in the wheel" who goes about her job without thinking or feeling. Summer is crazy, but it's a different crazy than the school year. To keep summertime intentional, we need to check our attitudes, as they will directly impact the temperament of the family.

Whatever the moment brings you, enjoy it! Whether the second hand seems to move too fast or too slow, stay connected with your family. An old hymn says, "Yesterday, today, forever, Jesus is the same. All may change, but Jesus never, glory to His name." He is forever faithful, present, and cheering you on.

Love and Blessings,
Daphne Close and the Help Club for Moms Team

> ❝ *Words can never adequately convey the incredible impact of our attitude toward life. The longer I live the more convinced I become that life is 10 percent what happens to us and 90 percent how we respond to it.* ❞
>
> ~ Chuck Swindoll

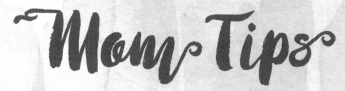

Mom Tips

By: Leslie Leonard

"When the righteous cry for help, the Lord hears and delivers them out of all their troubles. The Lord is near to the brokenhearted and saves the crushed in spirit." ~ Psalm 34:17-18 (ESV)

The Wise Woman Builds Her Spirit:

- Before getting out of bed every morning this week, turn your day over to God. Pray that He will provide for all your needs all day. Your job is to trust Him.

- Write Jeremiah 31:25 on your notecards or record it on your phone. Memorize the verse by the end of the week.

The Wise Woman Loves Her Husband:

- Take the week to organize your master bedroom. Declutter your nightstands, put away any laundry piles, and throw away trash. Take time to make your bedroom a sanctuary, a place of comfort and relaxation, not chaos. Make a personal commitment to keep the room tidy.

- Have your children write notes of love and encouragement to your husband this week and hide them in his work (or gym) bag.

The Wise Woman Loves Her Children:

- Create a "Chore/Bored Jar" for your children this week. Get some popsicle sticks and a mason jar and write down different activities on the sticks. On our sticks, we have some fun activities like "get out the paints" or "play-doh" and some easier chores like "sweep the kitchen" and "dust the baseboards." It's luck of the draw. You can choose if you have more fun or more chores—it's up to you!

- Invite neighborhood friends over for a water balloon fight/sprinkler party! What child doesn't love an afternoon running through the sprinklers? It's even better with a few friends.

The Wise Woman Cares For Her Home:

- Clean out under your kitchen sink this week. Take everything out and wipe the entire space. Throw away any garbage and any expired cleaning supplies. Organize the items as you put them back.

- Meal plan for the week. Know what is for dinner every day by 9:00 a.m. If you have meat in the freezer, take it out and put it in the refrigerator so you are not scrambling after school.

> "May God himself, the God of peace, sanctify you through and through. May your whole spirit, soul and body be kept blameless at the coming of our Lord Jesus Christ. The one who calls you is faithful, and he will do it."
>
> ~ 1 Thessalonians 5:23-24

Remember to Take Care of Yourself

By: Rachel Jones

Motherhood is exhausting. If I can be honest, it is a lot harder than I thought it would be. I am sure most of you can agree that the intensity of it all has been a surprise. The love for our children is intense, and so is their strong will to be their own person, the tiredness from trying to do everything, and the frustration that comes from spending all of our time caring for others.

It is hard. And that's why it's time to start caring for ourselves, mamas, because we cannot pour from an empty cup!

It's normal to get overwhelmed with the responsibility of being a mother, a wife, and a human. We spread ourselves so thin, taking care of everybody else but ourselves. But I'm here to tell you, mama, you need to take care of you too. In Matthew 11:28 Jesus calls to us, saying "Come to me, all you who are weary and burdened, and I will give you rest." He desires us to slow down and find a few tranquil moments with Him.

You are just as important as those babies that you spend every waking minute (and most sleeping ones too) worrying about. Your family is amazing, and they deserve the best version of you. Well, guess what? The best version of you will only be created if you take breaks! Love on yourself a bit and let Jesus do the heavy lifting. Psalm 55:22 says, "Cast your cares on the Lord and he will sustain you; he will never let the righteous be shaken." Go take a bubble bath, read a book, or go to Target and walk through every aisle alone.

Every mother is still her own person! Underneath all of the laundry, dishes, and lists, you're you, and you need to maintain that individuality in order to be fulfilled. Trust me, I've been there, and it's an empty feeling when you lose who you are. So go take a break, mama. It's okay. I'm taking one too.

Go Deeper:

• I strongly encourage you to spend some time in prayer about this topic. Read a few of these verses about your identity in Christ and be reminded of whose you are. You are more than a busy mom; you are a daughter of the King with gifts and talents that need to be cultivated and cherished!

  • Philippians 1:6 • 2 Timothy 1:7 • 1 Corinthians 3:16 • 1 Peter 2:5

What's Next?

Write in your journal or even on a whiteboard a few dreams or goals for yourself. I know this will be a challenge, but these cannot be related to your role as a wife or a mother. A few examples are reading goals, exercising goals, or goals of learning a language or an instrument. Something I am currently hoping and praying for myself is to have the diligence to regularly call my sisters. They both live out-of-state, and I know this would be wonderful for our relationship. Friends, I am praying for all of you!

journal

Week Three

> "...let us run with endurance the race that is set before us, looking to Jesus, the founder and perfecter of our faith, **who for the joy that was set before him endured the cross,** despising the shame, and is seated at the right hand of the throne of God."
>
> ~ Hebrews 12:1c-2 (ESV)

Enduring for the Joy

By: Katie Sadler

A wise woman endures.

Late nights *and* early mornings are not my cup of tea! I prefer the "early to bed; early to rise makes a man happy, healthy, and wise" motto! However, my children are young adults now and endurance is what I need most. Enduring the fatigue in order to steal a short download of their day or to grab a hug and tell them I love them as they run out the door is worth it!

So often I am reminded of how God conditioned me when my children were little. During the middle-of-the-night interruptions, God repeatedly spoke to my heart that they wouldn't be little for long and reminded me to relish the time even when it was hard. I'm so glad I heeded that lesson with babes, so I can again practice it with the young man and lady living under my roof.

Enduring means staying in the hard times: staying awake, staying accessible, staying alert, staying ready, staying the course. Endurance is staying when we want to retreat—when we want to throw in the towel, but deep down we know we should continue. Jesus endured the suffering of the cross because of "the joy set before Him" (Hebrews 12:2). You and me, we were the joy. Our being with Him throughout eternity was His joy. What is your joy? Why endure?

As you may be nursing a sick child or rocking an infant in the middle of the night, wishing it would all pass quickly—pray. Ask the Lord to remind you of the joy set before you in that situation. If young adults now pass through your door at all hours of the day and night, and if you are feeling fatigue suffocate your joy—pray. Ask the Lord to give you endurance to run the race.

Go Deeper:

• Is there a situation through which you know you need to endure? Take a few minutes and ask God to show you how to endure. Ask Him to show you the joy set before you as motivation to endure. Maybe you need to lean on His power and knowledge and just give it to Jesus to carry as you stand. He tells us in Matthew 11:29-30 (ESV), "Take my yoke upon you, and learn from me, for I am gentle and lowly in heart, and you will find rest for your souls. For my yoke is easy, and my burden is light."

What's Next?

This week, maybe you need to take a little time to find your reason for enduring. Grab a piece of paper and write down what the joy set before you is in your situation Put it where you will be reminded of it when it gets hard to endure. Maybe you simply need to recommit your resolve to endure. Whether you need endurance in your marriage, endurance to continually point your children toward the Lord, or endurance to finish the work project strong, it takes resolve and a clear picture of the joy set before you. Lean on the strong arms of Jesus and let the Holy Spirit lead you. Remember...the joy of the Lord is our strength (Nehemiah 8:10 ESV).

Week Three ~ Day Two

journal

_____
_____
_____
_____
_____
_____
_____
_____
_____
_____
_____
_____
_____
_____
_____
_____
_____
_____
_____
_____
_____
_____
_____
_____
_____

Guard your heart above all else, for it determines the course of your life. "

~ Proverbs 4:23 (NLT)

Be on Your Guard

By: Rebekah Measmer

Addiction. The word often makes us cringe as it implies a lack of self-control or carelessness. But the truth is that addictions are everywhere, even in our own homes. And it's okay, good even, to talk about them. For example, I struggle with a coffee addiction and had to give it up for several months because I was getting headaches if I didn't have at least one cup of coffee per day. Many of you (you know who you are) can empathize with that particular struggle!

I've always known that adults tussle with various cravings, but I learned recently that older children, particularly adolescents, are much more prone to addictions because their bodies produce higher levels of dopamine. Dopamine is a God-given neurotransmitter that helps control the brain's reward and pleasure centers. Now, I'm certain that few, if any, of your children have coffee addictions, but there are many types of addictions: food, television, video games (this includes iPads, iPhones, etc.), social media, and websites such as YouTube. And just as coffee isn't necessarily bad in small doses, none of these things are altogether bad, but they can be dangerous if we are unaware of the quality or impact of using them frequently.

The danger is that, if our children have higher levels of dopamine and are allowed to use the aforementioned potential addictions extensively, the neurotransmitter will give them a natural high, which will prompt them to desire more of what is giving them temporal pleasure. They will want to revisit them again and again, and if not moderated, this can cause lifelong dependencies.

> Be alert and of sober mind. Your enemy the devil prowls around like a roaring lion looking for someone to devour. (1 Peter 5:8)

Many young men and young women struggle with pornography addictions, some as young as early elementary age, and that number grows each year. Surprising? It shouldn't be. Pop-ups on otherwise inoffensive websites will confront our kids without any invitation. One curiosity-prompted click can lead to another, and another. A local Christian addiction expert stated that the second click indicates addiction. It happens that quickly, friends. We *must* be on our guard because our enemy is waiting for the opportunity to strike, regardless of age or innocence.

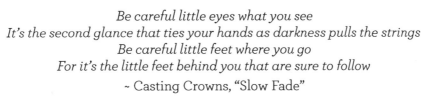

Be careful little eyes what you see
It's the second glance that ties your hands as darkness pulls the strings
Be careful little feet where you go
For it's the little feet behind you that are sure to follow
~ Casting Crowns, "Slow Fade"

Go Deeper:

- Are you so busy guarding your family's front door that you are not noticing the attacks of the enemy that sneak in through the back gate?

- Have you talked candidly with your children about guarding their minds, hearts, and bodies from the subtle attacks of the enemy? Are you guarding your own mind, heart, and body?

Week Three ~ Day Three

- Take the opportunity this summer to discuss these potential dangers with your family and come up with a plan to limit TV, internet use, and unhealthy binge-snacking.
  - Our family uses Media Tickets to regulate the use of electronics each week. Each child has 5 tickets for 30 minutes each (2.5 hours total) that can be used for G-rated video games, parent-approved movies, or commercial-free shows. We do not allow any TV or internet use without direct parental supervision. The tickets can all be used at once or throughout the week, but once they are used, that child's media time for the week is finished. This method works great for our family, but something else might work better for you. You do you!
  - To limit unhealthy snacking take the time to cut up fresh fruits and vegetables to have ready for quick snacks. If you buy crackers or chips, portion them out into snack baggies or small reusable containers.

What's Next?

Here are some resources worth looking into to keep your family pure of mind, heart, and body:

- *Teaching Your Children Healthy Sexuality* by Dr. Jim Burns
- *The Purity Code* by Dr. Jim Burns
- *Preparing Your Son for Every Man's Battle* by Stephen Arterburn, Fred Stoeker, with Mike Yorkey
- *Pursuing the Pearl* by Dannah Gresh
- *Lies Young Women Believe* by Dannah Gresh and Nancy Leigh DeMoss
- *Raising Body Confident Daughters: 8 Conversations to Have with Your Tween* by Dannah Gresh
- *It's Great To Be A Girl! A Guide To Your Changing Body* by Dannah Gresh and Suzy Weibel
- http://purefreedom.org/meet/dannah/

journal

_____
_____
_____
_____
_____
_____
_____
_____
_____
_____
_____

> " Be alert and of sober mind. Your enemy the devil
> prowls around like a roaring lion looking for someone to devour. "
>
> ~ 1 Peter 5:8

The Best Defense Is a Good Offense

By: Heather Doolittle

I used to believe the adage "the best defense is a good offense." It was really practical advice for a school-age kid. As I was growing up, bullies didn't generally pick on me because they would go for an easier target. Although it is not a godly way to live, I didn't know any better. Then, I grew up and became a Christian, which rendered all my past experience and advice useless when my kind-hearted daughter encountered a bully in second grade. I was at a loss for how to help her deal with it because my instinct just didn't seem to fit with what the Bible says. So instead, I told her to be kind anyway, and I tried to teach her better ways to cope with conflict. It didn't make her situation any better.

The bully made my daughter miserable every day, and unlike my daughter, she was good at shifting gears and acting super sweet in front of the teachers. At the same time, I volunteered in the classroom and saw how this girl struggled. She and my daughter were polar opposites, and my daughter excelled where she lacked (and vice versa). Even though my daughter couldn't fathom this popular girl with perfect hair being jealous of her, it was obvious to me that envy was the root of the constant bullying.

We made it through that season and learned valuable lessons that only come from heartache. However, it wasn't until much later that I figured out how I should have handled it: with spiritual warfare. You see, staying on the offense against your enemy is great advice, as long as you keep in mind who your real enemy is: Satan. "For we wrestle not against flesh and blood, but against principalities, against powers, against the rulers of the darkness of this world, against spiritual wickedness in high places" (Ephesians 6:12). If my daughter had taken the offensive against this other girl, God's precious child, the bullying might have stopped, but the other girl's envy and heartache would have increased.

Satan's goal is to destroy *all* of us in every way possible, but God tells us to rise above it and be righteous. By using her gifts of persuasion and good people skills the way she did, turning envy into pride and being cruel to others, this girl unwittingly continued down Satan's path and eventually fell from popularity, ruining what was good in her life. That is why Galatians 5:15 warns us, "If you bite and devour each other, watch out or you will be destroyed by each other." Your real enemy wants to use you to ruin others, and then he will take you down too. Satan had a similar plan for my daughter, but while she also sinned and messed up along the way, she prayed and *tried* to follow God. His path led her out of the strife to a place where she has grown. Now that she is removed from this situation, she has sympathy for her former enemy and has developed a soft spot in her heart for kids who don't fit in.

Bullies, antagonists, and enemies come and go from our lives, but we need to keep our footing on the firm foundation of absolute Truth. My younger daughter is now facing a bully in school, but it is much easier to handle now that we know what to do: "But I tell you love your enemies and pray for those who persecute you" (Matthew 5:44). Separate yourself from the toxic situation, believe the best about everyone, and pray for them. Believe that God is good and powerful, and He will ultimately work everything out for good if you stay on course (Romans 8:28).

Go Deeper:

- What are the difficult relationships in your life? Have you lost sight of the real enemy and who you are battling?

- Give these situations back to God. Confess how you have sinned, ask for forgiveness and guidance, and believe that God will help you. Just keep bringing it back to God.

What's Next?

Do your kids (or you) struggle with a troubled relationship that causes strife and drama? Use it as an opportunity to teach your children how to love their enemies. Read this study with them or find a children's book or devotion on the topic. Teach them to recognize Satan as the true enemy in the situation.

Teach them to believe the best about others; talk about the good characteristics of difficult people. Talk about why they might act that way. You don't have to know their backgrounds; just use your imagination to help your children see their enemies with a balanced perspective. Point out how your family doesn't act that way because of blessings from God: godly friends, a loving and supportive family, etc.

Teach them to rely on God for resolution. Pray for their enemies. Pray these people will grow into God's plan for their lives and learn how to behave, but also pray that they will prosper. Ask God to teach you and your family how to love these people and to see them the way God sees them.

Journal

_____

_____

_____

_____

_____

_____

_____

_____

_____

_____

_____

_____

_____

Food for the Soul

I just love salsa, and particularly in the summer! I am not talking about the kind you eat with chips, although I enjoy plenty of that during football season. I am talking about *fruit salsa*—sweet and tangy, and even sometimes with a little heat! Fruit salsa is perfect any time of year, but especially during the summer!

Allow me to share the most awesome salsa sundaes you will ever have! These are so easy that everyone reading this recipe can make them!

STRAWBERRY MANGO SALSA SUNDAES

By: Rae-Ellen Sanders

Ingredients:

2 cups strawberries, hulled and chopped

2 ripe mangoes (I use the frozen chunks from Trader Joe's)

1 tablespoon lime juice (freshly squeezed is always best)

12 burrito-sized soft white corn tortillas

½ cup sugar

1 tsp. cinnamon

4 tablespoons butter, melted

Strawberry syrup in a squeezable container

3 cups vanilla ice cream (at least) but more is always necessary for seconds!

Directions:

1. In a large bowl, hull and chop strawberries and mangoes. If using frozen mango chunks, defrost before chopping. If using fresh mangoes, peel before chopping.

2. Add freshly squeezed lime or 1 tbsp of bottled lime juice to fruit. Mix these ingredients together to allow flavors to marry. Refrigerate until ready to use.

3. Slice tortillas down the center, making 24 semi-circles.

4. Using pastry brush, brush melted butter on top. Combine cinnamon and sugar, and sprinkle the mixture liberally on both sides of the tortillas. If you end up needing more cinnamon sugar, repeat the process. I like them extra sugary!

5. Taking corners of tortilla, twist the tortilla into a cone shape, and press it into the cupcake/muffin pan. Corners should be resting outside the cup in a star shape.

6. Bake for 18 minutes at 350 degrees.

7. Remove from oven, and allow to cool on metal rack. Can you imagine that chunky sweetness with just a bit of tang spooned over vanilla ice cream? You are almost there!

STRAWBERRY MANGO SALSA SUNDAES

<u>(Directions Continued)</u>

8. When the tortillas are cool (and hardened), place on a plate. Add one scoop of your favorite ice cream, drizzle the strawberry syrup so that it runs down the sides, and finally (you guessed it), add your strawberry mango salsa on top for a refreshing treat!

Nothing is better in summertime than meat fresh off the grill, and when it is topped with fresh summer fruit & herbs—*yum*! As a bonus, below is my mango salsa recipe that is perfect for grilled meats and fish!

MANGO SALSA FOR FISH OR CHICKEN

By: Rae-Ellen Sanders

<u>Ingredients:</u>

1 to 2 large pitted and chopped mangoes

1 small red onion or half of a large one

1 lime – squeezed

¼ cup fresh cilantro, minced

1 red pepper, seeded and diced

1 small jalapeño, seeded and minced (optional)

a pinch of cayenne pepper

This salsa recipe is so easy! After you've made it once, I bet you can do it blindfolded—well, not the chopping part! It is just the right amount of sweet and heat to liven up any fish or chicken entrée!

<u>Directions:</u>

1. Combine chopped mango and onion, cilantro, cayenne pepper, and the juice from a squeezed lime.

2. Stir and refrigerate until ready to spread on top of your protein of choice.

Summer of Staying

~ Week Four ~

Hello Friends!

Lately, I've been pondering what it means to be present with my children. I am a stay-at-home mom, so that seems easy since I am with them a lot. However, they need much more than my physical presence; they need my attention and my heart. They need me to fight for them when they push me away (not literally fight, but maybe take them out for ice cream when I can barely stand to be around them). They need to see the love I feel from their sweet words and displays of affection as well as the joy I get from watching them learn and grow.

Summer provides us with plenty of opportunities to feed into our kids' hearts: picnics at the park, dollar movies, afternoons at the pool, planting gardens. Will you seize those opportunities to strengthen your relationships with your children? No pressure or Pinterest-perfect expectations— just stick around and engage in life with them. Model God's love for His children by showing that you adore them simply because they're yours. All the naughtiness and negativity will eventually fall away, and all the good behavior and sweetness is just icing on the cake.

This week, we will give some ideas on how to be present with your kids and take advantage of the time you have with them. I pray these studies are a blessing to you and your families, drawing your hearts closer to each other and to God!

Blessings and love,
Heather Doolittle and the Help Club for Moms Team

> ❝ *For the present is the point at which time touches eternity.* ❞
> ~ C.S. Lewis, *The Screwtape Letters*

Mom Tips

By: Leslie Leonard

"And let us not grow weary of doing good, for in due season we will reap, if we do not give up." ~ Galatians 6:9 (ESV)

The Wise Woman Builds Her Spirit:

- Plan to do all the Help Club for Moms Bible Studies this week. Summer gets busy, and we tend to let things slide. Schedule time on your calendar if you need to, but don't let the day end without doing your study.

- Pray in the car while doing your errands this week. Turn off the radio and tune into God. Speak out loud and pray the burdens that are currently in your heart and mind.

The Wise Woman Loves Her Husband:

- Work on getting rid of one habit your husband dislikes this week. Work on the steps it will take to completely remove it from your life. Pray for the strength and help to overcome the stronghold this "thing" has on your life.

- Tell your husband you love him every day this week. We sometimes neglect our spouses in the thick of parenting, work, and life. Really see him and tell him what he means to you.

The Wise Woman Loves Her Children:

- Pick two new kid-friendly recipes and have a "cook-off" competition between you and your children. Invite a grandparent or elderly neighbor over to be the celebrity judge.

- Encourage your children to keep Prayer Journals. They can write down their own prayer requests, as well as the prayer requests and praises of friends and family members. Remind them to follow up and write about how God answered the prayers. It's a great visual for children to see the love and power of God. If a child is not the best writer, pictures are a great start.

The Wise Woman Cares For Her Home:

- Brighten your home with flowers or a plant this week. A simple, inexpensive grocery store bouquet can brighten your kitchen table and bring you weeks of joy.

- Clear off all clutter from your dining room table. File or shred all paperwork, put away books, and find homes for wayward items. Commit to not using the dining room table as a dumping ground when you walk in the door.

Best Summer Ever

Bingo! for Moms!

5	37	28	35	7
33	14	40	23	34
11	2	47	16	20
49	42	9	12	48
26	19	31	8	22

-CARD ONE-

27	39	30	44	18
3	32	24	15	43
10	45	50	29	6
41	17	4	21	38
1	25	13	36	46

-CARD TWO-

Hey Mamas! Are you ready to have the best summer EVER and also win free prizes?

Join us for the HCFM's "Best Summer Ever Bingo!"

Here's how to play:

1. Print out "Best Summer Ever Bingo" printables

2. Pick activities to do and as you finish them, color in that number on the bingo square.

3. Each time you get a bingo, write "Bingo!" on Help Club for Mom's main Facebook page.

4. When you get a Blackout (all squares completed), write "Blackout!" on Help Club for Mom's main Facebook page.

5. Prizes will be given away for the first Bingo and the first Blackout!

6. Each Bingo will be entered into a drawing for **three** more prizes!

7. Ready? Set? Go!

Best Summer Ever

Bingo! for Moms!

1. Choose a hymn for each child and sing it with them
2. Share what you are learning in your Bible study with your kids
3. Lay on a blanket with your kids and look at stars
4. Color a picture with your child
5. Play a game of tag or hide and seek
6. Set up a small treasure hunt in your home or yard
7. Have a water balloon fight
8. Play outside with your kids
9. Read a book to your kids outdoors in the sunshine
10. Make a special treat together
11. Make something fun with a cardboard box
12. Make your child's favorite snack and go for a walk together
13. Do a science experiment
14. Make play-doh
15. Plant something with your kids—indoors or outdoors
16. Make paper airplanes and have a flying contest
17. Play pretend, use your imagination with your kids
18. Lay on the floor and play with your kids
19. Build something with your kids
20. Do an art project
21. Blow bubbles—homemade or store-bought
22. Run through the sprinkler together
23. Explore someplace new together
24. Paint rocks into animals
25. Read a Bible verse to your child and ask what they think
26. Turn on music and have a dance party
27. Tell your kids what you love about them
28. Make cards for family and friends and mail it
29. Visit someone who needs cheering up
30. Call grandparents together
31. Make a treat for a friend and deliver
32. Notice your kids strengths and point them out
33. Have a pretend circus or fair with your kids
34. Make a blanket fort
35. Do something to serve someone else together
36. Play "restaurant" with your child's favorite food, a menu, and fun decor
37. Have a talent show to showcase your kid's favorite talents.
38. Sing loud together, who cares about your voice
39. Dance and run around in a rain shower
40. Have a fancy meal at home
41. Go on a nature walk
42. Funny day—tell jokes and do things to make each other laugh
43. Snuggle each child longer than you normally would
44. Hug everyone today and express your love
45. Pray a verse for each child and your husband
46. Make a baking soda/vinegar volcano
47. Wash with your kids—use lots of bubbles
48. Stay up late with each kid, one at a time, and do something special
49. Play a card game in bed with your kids
50. Make ice cream sundaes

Best Summer Ever
Bingo! for Kids!

-CARD ONE-

38	12	29	35	48
6	33	46	27	13
19	50	2	44	21
42	7	11	30	18
25	16	23	9	4

-CARD TWO-

14	8	43	20	36
22	40	39	1	47
3	15	26	49	31
45	28	17	34	10
37	32	5	41	24

Hey Kids! Are you ready to have the best summer EVER and also win free prizes?

Join us for the HCFM's KIDS "Best Summer Ever Bingo!"

Here's how to play:

1. Print out "Best Summer Ever Bingo" printables

2. Pick activities to do and as you finish them, color in that number on the bingo square.

3. Each time you get a bingo, write "Bingo!" on Help Club for Mom's main Facebook page.

4. When you get a Blackout (all squares completed), write "Blackout!" on Help Club for Mom's main Facebook page.

5. Prizes will be given away for the first Bingo and the first Blackout!

6. Each Bingo will be entered into a drawing for **three** more prizes!

7. Ready? Set? Go!

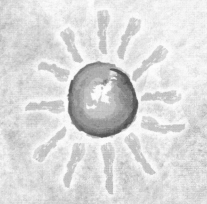

Best Summer Ever

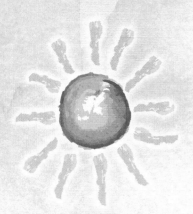

Bingo! for Kids!

1. Make your own board game
2. Tell someone about Jesus
3. Climb a tree
4. Look at the stars
5. Lay outside and watch the clouds (what shapes do you see)
6. Watch an insect or animal outside
7. Go for a walk
8. Make something for someone
9. Build a fort
10. Explore something new
11. Make your own adventure
12. Write a story (or have your parents write it down for you)
13. Make a special surprise for your parents
14. Tell your parents why you love them
15. Build something
16. Play outside
17. Make a new friend
18. Watch nature and draw a picture
19. Have a lemonade stand
20. Make an obstacle course
21. Make a snack or meal on your own
22. Draw a picture of your family
23. Do something to serve someone you love
24. Play a game of tag or hide and seek
25. Blow bubbles
26. Play pretend
27. Make something out of cardboard
28. Do something new
29. Look at books outside
30. Give your parents a foot or back rub
31. Learn a new song
32. Have a dance party
33. Do something kind for neighbor or friend
34. Draw a picture of a Bible story
35. Finger paint (use paint, shaving cream, or even chocolate syrup!)
36. Do something nice for your mom
37. Play a game outside
38. Go on an adventure—in your own home!
39. Play with water outdoors
40. Have a race
41. Do a science experiment
42. Make a circus or fair at home
43. Watch an insect or animal outside
44. Make your own adventure
45. Go for a walk
46. Blow bubbles
47. Play outside
48. Play a game outside
49. Do something new
50. Build something

> ❝Jesus replied: 'Love the Lord your God with all your heart and with all your soul and with all your mind. This is the first and greatest commandment.'❞
>
> ~ Matthew 22:37-38

What Is the Most Important Thing?

By: Kristi Valentine

Should I sign the kids up for golf lessons? What about camp? When do the in-laws arrive?

Sometimes summer can feel more stressful than the school year with all its activities, visitors, and vacations. I feel pressure to give my children as many opportunities as I can find on various blogs, Facebook, and online event calendars.

Truth is, I over schedule our family every single summer. Time management gurus challenge us to let go of busyness, follow a clear set of priorities, and say *no* more often. So, this summer, let's challenge ourselves: What are the most important things to do?

Actually, Jesus gave us the answer to this question thousands of years ago in Matthew 22. The most important thing to do in life is "to love God with all your heart and with all your soul and with all your mind." Translating this beautiful advice into my summer, I'm awakened to the need to prioritize God with my kids. Above golf. Above camp. Above all.

How do I make loving God more interesting to my children than jumping on the trampoline with the next-door neighbors? Here's what God has taught me to do:

- Every day, I write our family's top six priorities for the day on the chalkboard. Morning devotional time and daily Bible time always make the list. Next, I buy them each the same daily devotional book with short, kid-friendly topics, and before they emerge from their rooms for the day, they must complete their devos.

- Then, we do Bible time every day. I'm selective about which books of the Bible we walk through, so that it's as kid-friendly as possible. In our home, Bible time also means yummy treats like chocolate, ice cream, or cookies! Now my children ask to do Bible time every day!

Kids have a beautiful, innocent faith in God, and I am teaching them the spiritual discipline of spending time with God while they are young so that it lasts into adulthood. The best part is that my heart is joyful and at peace knowing I've impressed upon my children's hearts the most important thing: loving God with all their hearts, souls, and minds.

Go Deeper:

- Pray, pray, pray for your children to develop an authentic, rich love for God. Pray that for yourself too!

- Deuteronomy 6:5-7 says, "Love the Lord your God with all your heart and with all your soul and with all your strength. These commandments that I give you today are to be on your hearts. Impress them on your children. Talk about them when you sit at home and when you walk along the road, when you lie down and when you get up." Memorize this verse and let it motivate you to persist in seeking the things of God with your children every moment you can.

What's Next?

Find a kid's devotional book for each of your children to read every morning. Bible story coloring pages work great if the kids are still little. Remember, if a day is inadvertently missed, no worries and no guilt! Just pick up where you left off the next day and keep doing it!

Journal

_____

_____

_____

_____

_____

_____

_____

_____

_____

_____

_____

_____

_____

_____

_____

_____

_____

_____

_____

_____

_____

_____

_____

Week Four

> For I am confident of this, that He who began a good work
> in you will continue to perfect it until the day of Christ Jesus.
>
> ~ Philippians 1:6

"Mom, I Don't Think I Believe In God Anymore" & Other Mommy Nightmares

By: Deb Weakly

It's the stuff nightmares are made of.

Mom, I don't see anything wrong with getting drunk if you are old enough.

How do you know there is a God? He sure doesn't seem real to me!

If there is a God, why does Grandpa have cancer?

I don't think there is anything wrong with living together and not being married.

And the list goes on and on...

What do we do when our kids come to us with their doubts and questions? The first thing I would suggest is to stay calm and not blow a gasket!

Christian college chaplains have informed me that it is developmentally normal for teens and college-aged kids to wrestle with the questions of their faith. This is how they learn to own their own convictions. But it is a process of growth that may take some time.

Our daughter Christie once thought that God spoke to everyone but her. She felt like her quiet times were lifeless, and she never heard from God—ever. I remember praying and praying for God to speak to her and for her to learn how to hear God's voice.

By the grace of God, Christie was involved in an internship the summer of her 16th year in which the students and leaders went through the Bible study *Experiencing God*. That study really clicked with her and helped her learn how to hear God's voice for herself. Now, Christie loves God and hears from Him regularly. She has a depth to her soul that would not have been there had she not gone through her time of questioning.

If you have a teen or college student who may be going through a season of doubt, simply stay calm, pray, and trust God. Whatever happens, "Conduct yourselves in a manner worthy of the gospel of Christ" (Philippians 1:27). Don't blow up or freak out, and don't assume the worst of your kids.

Remind your kids that God loves them and tell them how much you admire their faith. Let your older kids know that their questions are okay because it shows that they are developing their own faith in God. Tell them how thankful you are that they come to you and trust you with their questions. Let them know that you believe in them and that God is leading them.

I have seen parents pray about their child's lack of faith in a negative way—within earshot of their kids. Please, please, never do that! Don't ever let your kids think that you believe they are lost, especially your adult kids. God will never let them go and wants none of them to perish.

Remember, the Holy Spirit has access to our children's hearts and minds and will be speaking to them. He will work in mysterious and miraculous ways!

> Being confident of this; that He who began a good work in you will carry it on to completion until the day of Christ Jesus. (Philippians 1:6)

God is working. He will never let your children go! Keep the lines of communication open and remember that if they don't come to you, they will most likely go to their friends or culture with their doubts. **You want them to come to you and know that you are always on their side and will always believe in them!** You serve a big God, and He is in love with your children and will pursue them all of their lives!

Go Deeper:

- Do you struggle with fear as a mom? What are your top three fears with your kids? Write them in your journal. Then, find a Bible verse that speaks to that fear.

  Here is one of my fears:

  I worried that because I wasn't raised in a Christian home, my kids would not grow up to love God. A verse that helped me was "All your children will be taught by the Lord, and great will be their peace" (Isaiah 54:13). I prayed this verse for my kids frequently. It helped me remember that God was the one who was in charge of teaching my kids to follow Him and that He would draw them to Himself.

What's Next?

As our kids were growing up, we loved celebrating! I purchased a "This is Your Day to Celebrate" plate from Pampered Chef to help birthdays and other fun days feel more special. Celebrate the anniversary of your kids' salvation and baptism dates to help them remember how they came to Christ.

Journal

_____

_____

_____

_____

_____

_____

_____

_____

Week Four

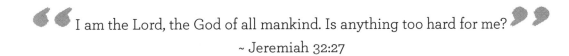

> ❝ I am the Lord, the God of all mankind. Is anything too hard for me? ❞
> ~ Jeremiah 32:27

Teaching Children That Nothing Is Impossible with God

By: Tara Davis

It is easy to forget that our children face trials in their lives just like we do. Regardless of age, life is never easy. Jesus desires to walk alongside our children through their challenging seasons! He wants them to rely on Him for strength and trust Him for the resolution in seemingly impossible circumstances. The Lord wants our children to know that, through Him, all things are possible (Matthew 19:26)!

This concept can be illustrated in a fun object lesson! The following experiment and devotional will demonstrate that even situations that appear nearly impossible can be made possible. God is our Abba Father, and He brings solutions to trials that seem too immense to be resolved in the lives of those who love Him.

To perform this experiment, you will need the following:

- a peeled hard-boiled egg
- a clean bottle or jar with an opening slightly smaller than the diameter of the egg
- boiling water (or simply heat the empty bottle with the egg in a pot of boiling water)

You will be using the heat of the boiling water to create pressure and suction, which will pull the egg through the mouth of the bottle. This method will take about 30-40 minutes, so it's great to do the devotional and then continue to check on your experiment until complete. For a more detailed scientific explanation of how this works, visit: http://chemistry.about.com/od/chemistrydemonstrations/a/egginabottle.htm

Have this conversation with your children as you perform the experiment:

"Let's try to fit this hard-boiled egg into our bottle! Can you do it without damaging the egg? No? It seems impossible, doesn't it? That egg is just too big! But, impossible things are not always as they seem. Let me show you how to make that egg easily fit through the opening of this bottle."

Pour a couple inches of boiling water into the bottle. Place the peeled egg firmly into the opening of the bottle. If the egg is much larger than the bottle, gently roll the egg between your palms to make it more slender. As you wait, continue your conversation.

"Have you ever had a problem in your life that seemed just too hard to be solved? We all find ourselves in difficult or sad situations at one time or another. But God is able to help us! Like the water in the bottle, Jesus is called our 'Living Water.' He is able to meet all of our needs, and He wants us to bring our problems and impossible situations to Him!"

Week Four

"How can you bring your problems to the Lord? You can pray and tell Him what is bothering you. In fact, you cannot pray too often. God wants to hear what you are feeling, He wants to help you, and He wants you to trust Him."

It may take a while for enough pressure to build up inside the bottle to pull the egg down. Use this as part of the object lesson.

"Sometimes, even when we are talking to God and trusting Him to help us work through our problems, things take longer than we would like. Just because you are waiting for a resolution to your problem, does not mean God isn't working. There are all sorts of things going on in this bottle right now that we cannot see and which will eventually help the egg pop into the bottle. Just because we cannot see things happening in our lives, does not mean that God is not at work helping us!

After the egg pops into the bottle, say:

"Look, it was possible after all! If we are able to make things happen that seem to be impossible, imagine how much more our *powerful God* will do in your life!

Let's see what the Bible says about this!"

Read Mark 10:27:

"With man this is impossible, but not with God; all things are possible with God" (Mark 10:27).

"When hard times come your way, will you trust the Lord to help you? Jesus loves you more than you could ever imagine. He wants you to talk to Him like you would your best friend. He is able to help you more than any friend on this earth ever could! He is able to make the impossible things possible in your life!"

Pray:

"Thank you, Lord, that you love us and that you are strong enough to help us with our problems. Help us to talk to you and trust you."

Questions to ask:

- Can you think of a time when a problem seemed too difficult to fix? Do you have any problems like that in your life right now?

- How can you trust God during hard times? Can you ask Him to help you? Can you talk to Him when you are worried? Let's pray together right now!

- For very young children, sing the song *My God is So Big* to remind them that nothing is impossible for God! If you do not know the song, look for it on YouTube.

Go Deeper:

- Have you struggled with your belief that God can do all things, that He is the Supreme Ruler over all and that His love for you is deeper than any other? Take some time to read Mark 9:14-29 and pray that God will strengthen your belief in Him and help you with your unbelief. God gives wisdom generously when we believe (James 1:5-8).

What's Next?

Find a time this week to talk to your kids about trusting God in both good times and bad. Your children need to learn about God's love and power from you!

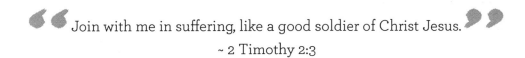

> **"** Join with me in suffering, like a good soldier of Christ Jesus. **"**
>
> ~ 2 Timothy 2:3

God Is Your Comforter

By: Kristall Willis

Recently, my son woke me up in the middle of the night, and I could not fall back asleep. As I lay there, my mind reeling from one thought to the next, hour after hour passing, I felt the Lord say to me: I have not created you to be comfortable in *this* world, for *this* is only temporary. True comfort will come only in the heavenly realms with me, in my Kingdom!

This thought is such a departure from the mentality I was raised with: if you follow the rules, work hard, and go to school, then you will be successful and therefore build a bubble of comfort around your life. I've found that mentality just does not pan out, unless you gauge comfort differently than I do!

See, do we look to the world's view and our financial standing as our security and comfort, or do we turn to God as our comforter?

> Praise be to the God and Father of our Lord Jesus Christ, the Father of compassion and the God of all comfort, who comforts us in all our troubles, so that we can comfort those in any trouble with the comfort we ourselves receive from God. (2 Corinthians 1:3-4)

Our worth is not dependent on our earthly successes or trials, for that matter. When we face trials in our lives, the natural human response is to freak out and ask, "Why is this happening and what did I do wrong?" The Lord did not promise us perfect lives here on earth, and no amount of hard work or goodness will guarantee your success here. Jesus said in Mark 8:34-35, "Whoever wants to be my disciple must deny themselves and take up their cross and follow me. For whoever wants to save their life will lose it, but whoever loses their life for me and for the gospel will save it."

When we face trials and suffering in this life, and we will, we should lean on God even more and allow Him to carry us through, for "...we also glory in our sufferings, because we know that suffering produces perseverance; perseverance, character; and character, hope" (Romans 5:3-4). It is a testing of our faith when we rely on God and glorify Him through our troubles (James 1:12). This will not be easy, but real growth happens here, in these hard times.

If you find yourself constantly being bombarded with one obstacle after the next, stand firm and reach for God! He seeks us out and desires our *whole* hearts, rather than us turning to Him secondarily after we decide, in our own strength, what is right or just. It's time we die to self and live for Him!

The Psalmist says that our lives on this earth are fleeting, just a mere handbreadth (Psalm 39:4a-5a). It is important that we make use of our short time here and find the Lord's calling for us (2 Peter 1:10-11). Once we figure that out, and follow His Spirit's guidance, we attain true success in our Father's eyes. How pleasing is it to have your Father smile down on you saying, "well done, good and faithful servant" (Matthew 25:21)!

Go Deeper:

- Has there been a time in your life when you have turned away from God because of hard times? Have you sought His counsel only after trying to operate on your own strength? Pray and ask the Lord to help you seek Him first and rely on Him for strength and perseverance through trials.

Week Four ~ Day Four

• Do you know what God is calling you to do for Him? If not, pray and ask Him to send His Spirit to guide you and open doors to do His kingdom work.

What's Next?

This week, be intentional about turning to God first when faced with adversity or suffering. Seek Him out by praying first before making any decisions.

If you find yourself relying on your own strength, just stop and pray for His will to be done and ask for clarity in that situation.

Lastly, listen to "Good Good Father" by Chris Tomlin. https://youtu.be/iBmwwwiHrOk

Thank the Lord for how He has worked in your life and how He has guided you.

journal

Summer of Staying

~ Week Five ~

Hello My Friend,

It's hard to believe we're already beginning week five of our study! I'm curious as to what God is showing you—what you're learning!

How's your summer going? I hope you're in full swing, enjoying the warm summer evenings, picnics, watermelon, and hot dogs or marshmallows roasted over an open fire. It's a wonderful time to make fun memories with your precious family.

I love, love summertime and the spontaneous freedom that comes along with it—no school or homework for the children makes for less stress and more rest for mama! Yay for sleeping in!

Whatever you're doing or feeling about yourself this very moment, always remember you'll greatly treasure the time you spend with your loved ones. All the effort is worth it! Someday, you'll look back with a grateful heart. God picked you to be the mama for your kids; it was His idea. He knew you were the perfect one for them. Don't look back at past mistakes you've made, but look up to your Creator and ask Him to give you vision for the future. God's thoughts toward you are simply amazing, His ideas are better than you can imagine! Trust Him. Always know that He believes in you!

Blessings and love,
Mari Jo Mast and the Help Club for Moms Team

> 66 *Spending time with God through prayer and His Word is a prerequisite for having a great life and fulfilling your purpose.* 99
>
> ~ Joyce Meyer

By: Leslie Leonard

"For nothing will be impossible with God."
~ Luke 1:37 (ESV)

The Wise Woman Builds Her Spirit:

- Pray first thing in the morning and last thing in the evening every day this week. Start and finish your day with God.

- Memorize Colossians 3:23. Write it on your chalkboard or notecards or record it on your phone. Try to have it memorized by the end of the week.

The Wise Woman Loves Her Husband:

- Plan a date night out. Get out of the house with your husband and without the children. Head somewhere you always talk about trying but never do, OR try something you would never try in 100 years. If you can't decide, put a few choices in a bowl and draw a winner.

- Start a couples devotion time together. You can start reading the same book in the Bible or choose a study book to go through together. Set aside time each week dedicated to Bible Study.

The Wise Woman Loves Her Children:

- Let your children stay up late one evening to stargaze. While outside, teach them Psalm 136:7-9.

- Get your children involved in making dinner this week. Let them help get the family meal prepared, and ask them to set the table. Ask one of your children to pray over the family meal.

The Wise Woman Cares For Her Home:

- Clean out your pantry this week. Wipe down all surfaces and check expiration and "use by" dates on packages. Organize all items as you put them away.

- Eat from your food pantry and freezer this week. Be creative and see what you can use up without going to the grocery store.

> ❝ He humbled you, causing you to hunger and then feeding you manna, which neither you nor your ancestors had known, to teach you that man does not live by bread alone but on every word that comes from the mouth of the Lord. ❞
>
> ~ Deuteronomy 8:3

I'm Hungry

By: Julie Maegdlin

How many of you wake up in the morning hungry for breakfast? When my girls were younger, I was always up early to make sure that they were properly fed before they started their days. I have always known the importance of a good breakfast.

Can you imagine telling your family that they can't eat?

God did. As a matter of fact, He made sure that His people were good and hungry before He gave them manna. Why? He did it to teach them the importance of relying on Him and His Word.

If God was willing to let His people go hungry for a period of time, then it must have been for a pretty important reason. He wants to teach us that His Word is essential for our lives. The Word of God is so important to know that God was willing to let the Israelites suffer in order to learn this lesson.

The Word of God is essential for our lives. But how can we get to know it better? One of the first things to do is to understand that our loving Father gave us His Word to help us. It isn't a to-do list, it is a love letter. It is God's revelation of Himself. God wants us to get to know Him through His Word. He even promises blessings to us when we get to know Him better! Matthew 5:6 says that we are blessed (happy) when we hunger and thirst for righteousness. He will fill us up.

God also promises to guide us through His Word. Psalm 119:105 says that His Word is a lamp for our feet and light for our path. I know that I can get lost very easily. Who knows where I would be without my GPS? God's Word is our spiritual GPS. God knows where we are, and He knows how to get us to where we are going.

God loves you so much! He wants to bless you. He tells us in many places in Scripture what we must do for His blessings. Luke 11:28 tells us that all we have to do is, "hear and keep the word of God." Jesus tells the crowds in Capernaum that God wants us to simply, "believe in him whom he has sent" (John 6:29).

Isn't that amazing? Our Father, the Creator of the heavens and the earth, has written us a love letter. He gives it to us so that He can teach us and so that we can learn how to do things correctly. He wants to train us in righteousness, and gives the Word to us to make sure that we are complete and equipped for every good work (2 Timothy 3:16-17). He longs to teach us and have us get to know Him in a very deep way. He even promises to manifest Himself to those who accept His commandments and obey them (John 14:21 NLT)!

Go Deeper:
- Have you ever looked at the Bible as your personal GPS? Do you need clarity on which direction to go? I love that God not only knows everything about us from before we were created in our mother's wombs, but also that He goes before us! He has all the answers!

What's Next?

Ask the Lord for a renewed hunger to read and digest His Word. Place your plans and hopes in God's hands, and ask Him to line up your heart's desire with His perfect plan for your life! Encourage your children to seek the Lord for answers to the questions they have too—which university to go to, which career should they should choose, etc. Then, point them to the Scriptures as the source for all the wisdom they need. I encourage you to seek God for every step you take and draw ever so near to Him in the process.

Journal

_____

_____

_____

_____

_____

_____

_____

_____

_____

_____

_____

_____

_____

_____

_____

_____

_____

_____

_____

_____

_____

Week Five

> " I am the true vine, and My Father is the vinedresser. Every branch in Me that does not bear fruit He takes away; and every branch that bears fruit He prunes, that it may bear more fruit. You are already clean because of the word, which I have spoken to you. Abide in Me, and I in you. As the branch cannot bear fruit of itself, unless it abides in the vine, neither can you, unless you abide in Me. 'I am the vine, you are the branches. He who abides in Me, and I in him, bears much fruit; for without Me you can do nothing.' "
>
> ~ John 15:1-6 (NKJV)

The Wise Woman Stays Connected

By: Rae-Ellen Sanders

Today, we are going to dig up Scriptures that are sure to affirm your growth in the Lord. Read John 15:1-6 above. Don't forget your gardening tools! We are going to take a look at staying connected to the Vine, how to be planted to grow to bear fruit, and how to accept the pruning shears as a method of correction for our betterment.

Good News: God wants to create a beautiful garden through you! He desires for each of us to reap a flourishing life that leads to an extravagant, eternal harvest! Our Christian life, just like a summer garden, involves necessary pruning that is never enjoyable for the gardener or the plant but yields fruit. Spiritual pruning is a process that God uses in our lives to refine us. Just like discipline that we introduce to our children for their good, God prunes us daily, molding us to be more like Him.

Let's look at the garden of our souls. First, we need the essentials for growth:
- Healthy, rich soil to grow in (the body of Christ)
- The Living Water (Jesus) to nourish us with the truth daily
- Time spent with the Son (the Word of God)
- The Master Gardener (Jesus) to fight off the pestilence and cover us with His protection

As we read God's Word, we store it up, listen to its instruction, repent, believe, and obey. This moldable heart is the rich soil that the Word roots itself in, subsequently producing growth and eventual fruit. This heart delights in the law of the Lord! Read Psalm 1:1-4. This Scripture tells us a blessed man or woman meditates on the Word and will be like a tree planted by rivers of water that will bring forth fruit in season! According to Galatians 5:22, the **fruit** of the Spirit is love, joy, peace, longsuffering, kindness, goodness, faithfulness, gentleness, and self-control. These fruits are cultivated and matured as we stay connected. They take time to grow and bloom in our lives; they won't just spring up overnight!

God's Word is food for our souls! If you have difficulty loving the Word of God, humble yourself and ask God to illuminate His Word so that it penetrates your heart. Don't be distracted. Repent that you haven't taken His word seriously and affirm you want to do what is *right*! God *wants* to produce a harvest of righteousness in your life!

Romans 10:17 says, **"faith *comes* by hearing, and hearing by the word of God."** Nurture the seeds of faith by listening to God's Word, by doing personal reading and meditation, or by listening to sermons, podcasts and/or praise music.

Week Five ~ Day Two

When we receive God's Word and understand it, it will produce fruit in our lives (Matthew 13:23). In fact, God says that He will know us by our fruits (Matthew 12:33)! Jeremiah 17:10 (KJV) says, "I the Lord search the heart, I *try* the reins, even to give every man according to his ways, *and* according to the **fruit** of his doings." The "doing" part is the fruitful part!

Go Deeper:

- Read the parable of the Seed & The Sower in Luke 8:11-15 and pay special attention to verses 14-15. The thorns that choke our fruit are the cares of the world and our seeking after the pleasures of life. Be conscious of what vies for your attention or keeps you from staying connected to Jesus.

- Seek the Lord and allow God's Words to abide in you! Remember that you don't grow fruit in isolation; surround yourself with other believers in Bible Study, prayer, and church! Bearing fruit is also about being a blessing to others in the name of Jesus. May you yield abundant fruit as you blossom and mature in the garden of the body of Christ.

> By this My Father is glorified, that you bear much fruit; so you will be My disciples. (John 15:8)

What's Next?

How much time do you spend soaking up the strength of God's presence? Will your leaves wither when storms come? Seeking God daily will grow you up and keep your eyes on Him! Are your branches bearing fruit? God wants to deal with the root of the problem, not the fruit of the problem. Surrender any toxic soil that you are rooted in. Ask the Lord to prune areas that need it. The Bible plainly states that if a tree is bad, it will bear bad fruit; but if it is good, it will bear good. God *will* cut down every bad tree and throw it in the fire (Matthew 7:16-20)! Matthew 3:10 states that even now the ax is laid at the root of the trees. Don't allow the enemy to snatch your fruit! Stay connected to the Vine!

Week Five

Journal

_____

_____

_____

_____

_____

_____

_____

_____

> " How much better is your love than wine,
> and the fragrance of your oils than any spice! "
>
> ~ Song of Solomon 4:10

Weeding and Watering Your Garden

By: Rebekah Measmer

"Marriages either move toward connection, communication, and intimacy or they move away from those things—they don't 'stand still' for very long." – Unknown

When my husband and I were first married, we delighted in one another and the closeness we shared in the bedroom. Intimacy was exciting and mystifying. I had never felt as alive as when I was in my husband's arms and he was in mine. Though, in just a few short years' time, the excitement had waned. Sex, for me, became an inconvenience. No longer feeling like the beautiful sensual woman that my husband had married, I hid in the dark beneath the covers each night with my suggestive lingerie hidden in the depths of my closet.

What had happened? In short, three ugly weeds had grown in our garden of intimacy and were strangling the flowers of love, faith, and selflessness. Over time, with many hours devoted to Biblical books on intimacy and wise Christian counsel from godly men and women, God revealed each of these "weeds" in our marriage and began to renew my thinking and my heart.

The first weed was insecurity. The thought of standing uncovered before the man I married with my post-pregnancy stretch marks, deflated breasts, and added 'muffin top' made me unsure of myself. This insecurity weed propagated the second weed—fear. Afraid that my husband would no longer find me desirable, I remained hidden and refused to have sex with the lights on or during the day when he might see my self-proclaimed flaws. Needless to say, this took much of the excitement and spontaneity out of our marriage. Self-pity was the final weed. I not only pitied the absence of my pre-baby body but also pitied how tired I was from chasing children, cleaning house, doing laundry, cooking meals, etc. How could I be expected to have sex after *hours* of self-sacrifice?

When weeds sprout in your marriage garden, they must be removed by the Master Gardener. To remove insecurity, I had to receive and believe what the Bible proclaimed about me, and what my husband had been saying all along: I am truly beautiful; flawless (Song of Solomon 4:7). And, I had to repeat that truth to myself whenever I was tempted to think the opposite. When addressing fear, I prayed for boldness and surprised my husband by excavating the satin and lace out of the back of my closet and initiating sex *with* the lights on (Song of Solomon 3:4). Girls, men connect with who or what they are looking at during intercourse. Let him look at you—*all* of you! Finally, I had to ban self-pity, with its *I'm too tired* excuse, from my vocabulary. Unexpectedly, I found that if I welcomed my husband's attention in our bedroom, it took very little time for me to enjoy myself and forget how tired I had felt.

Mama, perhaps your weeds are different than mine. Shame. Betrayal. Depression. Weeds can take many forms, but they all choke the life out of the beautiful flowers God intended to grow in each of our marriage beds. Regardless of whether your garden has become a barren desert or a flourishing rainforest, I want to encourage you to pray for God to bless the intimacy in your marriage. Ask God for ideas on how to pursue your husband both in and out of the bedroom. Water your garden of intimacy—removing any weeds you find—and see what grows! You may be pleasantly surprised at the results.

Go Deeper:

- Read the Song of Solomon written by King Solomon the Wise.
- Make intimacy in your marriage a priority.

  Do not deprive each other except perhaps by mutual consent and for a time, so that you may devote yourselves to prayer. Then come together again so that Satan will not tempt you because of your lack of self-control. (1 Corinthians 7:5)

What's Next?

Add one of these books to your summer reading list.

- *Intended for Pleasure* by Ed Wheat, MD and Gaye Wheat
- *Intimate Issues* by Linda Dillow and Lorraine Pintus
- *Intimacy: A 100 Day Guide to Lasting Relationships* by Douglas Weiss
- *Love and Respect* by Dr. Emerson Eggerichs

Journal

_____

_____

_____

_____

_____

_____

_____

_____

_____

_____

_____

_____

_____

_____

_____

_____

_____

_____

Week Five

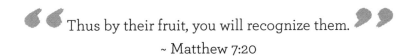

> Thus by their fruit, you will recognize them.
>
> ~ Matthew 7:20

Cultivating a Garden of Faith

By: Pam Mays

I love the simple joys of summer! It signals the end of the school year, a lighter schedule, and possibly a vacation or two. It is also a time of fresh, bountiful harvest, or it can be. I just love the fresh fruits and vegetables that are available during the summer months! When we lived in Georgia, I wanted to grow a garden. Having never lived in the deep south, I started planting my garden in April and looked forward to a plentiful harvest. Boy, was I disappointed! I didn't do enough research to know that you need to plant your garden in February and early March due to the intense heat that begins in May, thus, no harvest that year.

Planting a garden is much like our faith. Although it may seem fruitless at times, it is rooted in our salvation through Jesus Christ. 2 Kings 19:30 states, "Once more a remnant of the Kingdom of Judah will take root below and bear fruit above. And our fruit blossoms from that root of salvation." Our lives in Christ begin at salvation, and grow through prayer, spending time in His Word, and fellowshipping with other believers. Sometimes, even though we think we are doing the right things, it doesn't feel like there is fruit. If we fail to plant seeds in our soul through prayer and spending time in God's Word, those deep roots and fruit may never materialize.

What could help you cultivate deep roots and a fruitful harvest in your relationship with God?

Secure your gift of salvation. First and foremost, have you asked Jesus to be your Savior and Lord? If not, join me in prayer, "Father God, I come to you now. I know I am a sinner. Please forgive me for all my sins and make me brand new. I believe Jesus is your Son. I believe that He died for my sin and that you raised him to life. I want to trust Him as my Savior and follow Him as Lord. Fill me with your peace, hope, joy, and blessed assurance, so that you may be glorified."

Spend time reading the Bible. I recommend starting with the book of John. If you do not have a Bible, ask someone who you know is a believer to help you pick out a Bible and tell that person that you accepted Jesus as Lord of your life.

Seek a spiritual mentor. Pray and ask God to bring you a spiritual mentor with whom you can meet over the phone or in person at least once a month. Share the exciting things God is doing in your life, as well as the challenges that will come your way. Know that this will be a lifelong journey.

Congratulations, and welcome to the family! If you already know God, but are feeling far away from Him, just ask God to renew your relationship. In either case, He promises to never leave you or forsake you (Deuteronomy 31:6)!

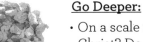

Go Deeper:

- On a scale from one to ten, how would you rate your relationship with Jesus Christ? Do you feel close to Him or do you feel far away? Talk to God about it. He wants you to stay close to Him and not do anything on your own. Read John 15.

Week Five ~ Day Four

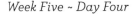

What's Next?

Who do you know who you can talk to about your relationship with Christ? We are not meant to go through life alone. If you don't know anyone who is a Christian, you can join the Help Club for Moms online group on Facebook. You will find plenty of Christian friends there!

Journal

_____

_____

_____

_____

_____

_____

_____

_____

_____

_____

_____

_____

_____

_____

_____

_____

_____

_____

_____

_____

_____

Week Five

Food for the Soul

Sometimes, I don't want to cook in the summer because it makes my house so hot! I have a great, hearty meal for you that goes in your slow cooker and has that great, slow-cooked taste without adding extra heat to your house.

Cooking a roast in a slow cooker also requires you to start it in the morning. You get a lot of the work out of the way early, leaving those busy summer evenings more open.

Acts 2:46 says, "They broke bread together and ate in their homes with glad and sincere hearts." Invite friends over for dinner, have them stay a while, and fellowship.

Quick Mom Tip: I buy my roasts when they are marked down at the grocery store and freeze them right away until I'm ready to use them. This is a great way to save money on a large chunk of meat.

FRENCH DIP SANDWICHES By: Brandi Carson

Ingredients:

3.5 lb (at least) beef roast, bone-in is best, but any cut will work

32-64 ounces of beef broth, depending on the size of roast used

1-2 tablespoons Beef Better than Bouillon—1 for a small box of broth, 2 for a large box of broth

½-1 teaspoon garlic powder, use generously

½-1 teaspoon onion powder, use generously

1-2 teaspoons crushed rosemary, divided

salt and pepper, season to taste

olive oil for coating

6-12 hoagie buns

Optional ingredients for toppings:

provolone cheese slices

yellow onions, 1-2 large, thinly sliced

mushrooms, 8-16 ounces of your favorite variety, sliced ⅓ inch thick

Directions for Cooking Roast:

1. Heat heavy-bottomed pan on medium-high heat—cast iron is great if you have it. While pan is heating, thoroughly coat roast with oil, and season generously with salt, pepper, garlic powder, and half of the crushed rosemary. The larger the roast, the more of the seasoning it will need. Reserve the other half of rosemary for broth.

2. Sear each side of roast until caramelized and golden brown on each side.

3. While roast is searing, place beef broth, remaining rosemary, and beef bouillon in the slow cooker. Be sure to dissolve all bouillon in broth.

4. When roast is seared on all sides, place in slow cooker with broth mixture. Place lid on and cook on low heat for 6-8 hours or high for 4-6 hours. Larger roasts will take more time, so plan accordingly. The roast will be done when the meat is falling apart.

FRENCH DIP SANDWICHES (Continued)

<u>Directions for Preparing Toppings:</u>

You can do prep work for most of the toppings in the morning while the roast is searing. You will just need to warm up the onions and mushrooms that evening.

Caramelized Onions

Cut onions in half and slice them as thinly as possible. Heat a large sauté pan, or Dutch oven, to medium-low heat. Add a generous amount of olive oil to the pan, and then add the onions to the pan, breaking them up. Stir occasionally until they are completely softened and begin to turn brownish in color. This can take 20-40 minutes, depending on the amount of onions.

Sautéed Mushrooms

Slice mushrooms to a good medium thickness, about ⅓ inch. Do not cut too thin or too thick Heat your sauté pan to a little higher than medium heat. Use cast iron if possible. Add a generous drizzle of olive oil to your pan, coating the bottom well. Now in my best Julia Child's voice, I say, "Don't crowd the pan!" Begin adding your mushrooms a little at a time. The goal is to only have a single layer of mushrooms without too much touching to prevent them from getting squishy. Cook the mushrooms in batches, or even use a couple pans at the same time. When you see the mushrooms browning on one side, turn them over. Cook them a little on the other side until they are browned. Remove from pan, and repeat with the next batch until all mushrooms are cooked, making sure you oil the pan generously between batches.

Now you are all prepped and ready to assemble your sandwiches!

1. Remove roast from slow cooker, allowing as much of the broth to drip off the roast as possible. Set aside and allow to cool.

2. While meat is cooling, strain broth from any bits that may remain in it. Set broth aside for the dip.

3. Shred roast once it is cool enough to handle. Season to taste with salt and pepper.

4. Slice hoagie buns in half, keeping the top and bottom intact on one side, if possible. This helps keep all the yummy filling in when the sandwich is being dipped in the broth.

5. Lay buns butterflied open and broil in the oven for a few minutes until browned. Remove from oven.

6. Add shredded roast on one side of the bun and any desired toppings. Add provolone slices to the other side. Be sure to cover bun to keep it from burning when broiled.

7. Place back under broiler until cheese is melted and bubbly. Remove from oven, close sandwich, slice diagonally in half, and serve alongside a bowl of broth for dipping.

Summer of Staying

~ Week Six ~

Dear Sister,

I hope your summer has been fun so far! I am excited that you are nurturing your soul with *The Wise Woman Stays* studies and being encouraged to keep God first in your life!

The summer months tend to go by so quickly, don't they? It's summer vacation for the kids after all. You're probably super busy hustling them here and there. It's easy to be preoccupied and satisfied with bare minimums when life is demanding. Summertime can easily become the stretch when we let our daily devotions and time with God fall to the wayside. Don't forget to stoke up the flames of your faith!

I once was a flip flop wearing mama. Sand in my car was an everyday occurrence, or rather a nuisance. We lived 30 minutes from the ocean, and I remember the first summer we moved to the mountains... We were so cold that we didn't turn the air conditioning on once, even in the heat of a Colorado summer! In fact, the summer we relocated across country, there were forest fires due to how dry it was, but we were freezing! It's interesting how our bodies adapt to where we live. Four years later, we now consider 55 degrees warm in the winter, 80 degrees hot, a sunny 34-degree day bearable, and 68 degrees just perfect! Instead of sand and beach toys, I now tote an extra jacket, water bottles, and granola bars!

No matter where you live, you eventually adapt to your environment, we all do. The question is: what kind of spiritual environment are you living in? How comfortable or complacent have you become in your walk with the Lord?

The Bible says in Revelation 3:15-16, "I know your deeds, that you are neither cold nor hot. I wish you were either one or the other! So, because you are lukewarm—neither hot nor cold—I am about to spit you out of my mouth."

Allow the book of Revelation to wake you up and give you a reality check in your spirit for where you are—hot, cold, or perhaps lukewarm? Maybe you need to start a new routine of putting Christ first in your life. Make a decision today to make the most out of the rest of the summer. Be set apart to become a *hot* mama for Jesus!

Blessings and love,
Rae-Ellen Sanders and the Help Club for Moms Team

> "*Put your nose into the Bible every day. It is your spiritual food.*
> *And then share it. Make a vow not to be a lukewarm Christian.*"
>
> ~ Kirk Cameron

Mom Tips

By: Leslie Leonard

"It is the Lord who goes before you. He will be with you; he will not leave you or forsake you. Do not fear or be dismayed"
~ Deuteronomy 31:8 (ESV)

The Wise Woman Builds Her Spirit:

- Would you like an easy way to organize your prayers? We love the idea of having a prayer binder. It's an easy way to keep all your prayers at your fingertips and will help you to create a lifelong habit of prayer.

- Work on your Prayer Binder this week. Step-by-step instructions are located on our website at www.helpclubformoms.com. Look under the "Getting Started" tab and click Special Topics.

The Wise Woman Loves Her Husband:

- Be reliable for your husband this week. Follow through on your commitments to him and your family. Don't over commit and allow for scheduling conflicts that bring strife into your home.

- Allow your husband to have a few minutes of alone time when he gets home from work to decompress from the day. He can "take off" the work day and be open to all the family has to give him in the evening hours.

The Wise Woman Loves Her Children:

- Start a morning devotion time with your children during breakfast. Choose a child-appropriate devotional book or Bible story book, and read it while your children are eating. Keep it short: you do not want this to cause you stress and delay.

- Have your children memorize Ephesians 4:32. Remind them to always choose to be kind to one another.

The Wise Woman Cares For Her Home:

- Choose to do a "no-spending" week or even a month. Besides your budgeted bills and groceries, don't spend any money. Go out of your way to NOT spend. See what you can save and what you can cut out. It's a good challenge and really eye-opening.

- Clean out your oven and microwave this week. Give both appliances a really deep cleaning, giving attention to all grooves.

" For our light and momentary troubles are achieving for us an eternal glory that far outweighs them all. "

~ 2 Corinthians 4:17

"No One Said This Would Be Easy"

By: Heather Doolittle

The other day, I was talking to the mom of a 16-year-old, and she was telling me about her child's current behavioral issues. I have no experience dealing with a rebellious teen, so I just offered encouragement and prayer. Then she made a comment about teens being difficult. Afterward, my 13-year-old told me that she will be an easy teenager since she was such a difficult little kid. Her words were true and her sentiment sweet, but something about that proclamation just didn't sit well with me. I pondered the conversation for a while, surprised that my daughter views herself that way. I came to realize there were two reasons why.

First, those hard years were harder on her than they were on me. She had a lot of struggles, and it broke my heart to see my innocent little girl constantly struggling. Yes, at the end of the day, she was cranky and rude to me, but anyone would be. I didn't want her to feel as though she had already used up her allotment of grace. In her difficult time, she grew in strength, grace, and compassion; and I want her to know I hold nothing against her for that.

Secondly, having easy children is not the goal of parenting. I didn't have kids to make my life easier. Raising my children has been *hard*; they have caused me immense struggle and heartache. They have brought me to my knees in prayer, but that is a *good thing*. I needed to grow and change. As a result, I can be not only a better parent but also a kinder, more patient person now.

I want my daughters to be bold and strong. I don't know what they will face in life, but I know that they will face it with the strength and courage that God is already cultivating in them. The present struggles and pain are refining them in a way that coasting through life never could. "For our light and momentary troubles are achieving for us an eternal glory that far outweighs them all" (2 Corinthians 4:17). If we want to prepare our children for greatness in whatever they do, we must teach them that the road will not be smooth, but it is worth the struggle for the eternal glory to come.

Children face constant pressure to be who the *world* wants them to be, so as their moms, we need to reaffirm that we love them and appreciate who God *made* them to be, for "[they] are his workmanship, created in Christ Jesus for good works, which God prepared beforehand, that we should walk in them" (Ephesians 2:10 ESV). In God's goodness, He created each of His children with a purpose, and He gave us everything we need to succeed in that purpose. We must shed light on our children's gifts; after years of cultivation, those very assets will be what sets them apart as adults. We must remind them that God created them just as they are with a very specific purpose.

After pondering my conversation with my daughter for a few days, I invited her for some alone time and told her what I am sharing with you. While her comment wasn't out of a place of hurt, nor was it significant to her, I think it was important to have this conversation to reaffirm that I see her heart, and it is beautiful. I hope that, if you have been struggling with a "difficult" child, or if you have seen them struggling in the world, this message will encourage you to take heart and keep your long-term goals in mind. God made our children the way he wanted them to be with just the right skills to fit into His perfect plan for their futures. We need to observe our children and learn their strengths and

Week Six

gifts in order to encourage them and steer them down the path God has laid out before them. We need to remind them that God, their loving Father, has set them apart for greatness (Jeremiah 1:5).

Go Deeper:

- Do you have a difficult child or one who's going through a difficult season? Have you said or done anything to inadvertently crush his or her spirit? If so, let go of any condemnation from Satan, repent, and ask God to show you how to do better.

- What can you do to reaffirm your children's value and help them grow into God's plan for their lives? How can you help them recognize their gifts?

What's Next?

For each of your children, make a list of their best qualities, and make it a point to mention them in conversation over the next few days. If you can't see it because of a strained relationship or difficult season, don't worry; I've been there too. Ask God to remove any bitterness you may have toward them and to help you love them and see the best in them.

Journal

_____

_____

_____

_____

_____

_____

_____

_____

_____

_____

_____

_____

_____

_____

_____

_____

_____

> " Come near to God, and he will come near to you.
> Humble yourselves before the Lord, and he will lift you up. "
>
> ~ James 4:8,10

When People Talk

By: Christie Frieg

I'll admit—I might have received a piece of discouraging information recently. That's normal, right? I feel like it is. And it hurt! What that person said about me made me feel like a hopeless case. I struggled with questions of how I should react. How much of it is true and how much is false? Should I continue to let it affect me? Am I *really* the way that person says I am?

However, this time I'm truly excited to share. You know why? Because I did the right thing the first time! That doesn't normally happen to me! Just kidding. Kind of...

When I received the piece of criticism, I sat in my bed for about ten minutes with my fingers poised above the keyboard, speechless about how to respond. What I read really hurt my feelings and caused me to question myself and feel like a terrible person. I decided not to respond just then. Instead, I grabbed my Bible and journal, made my way to my favorite quiet time spot with some tea, and sat down to process.

I began by telling God what was said about me. I then wrote how I felt about it and what my questions were for God. I asked Him to speak to me, and then began to read the New Testament. I read lots of verses about wisdom and humility (which was part of the criticism I received). Two verses from the book of James (James 3:17-18 and James 4:8-10) really stuck out to me.

From these verses, I confessed to God that I need to humble myself; I had not been conducting myself in a wise way. I was not seeking peace above all else. I was not being considerate or impartial, although I wanted to be those things. I accepted the words of criticism in this area as conviction, and I repented, promising God I would fight those tendencies and try my best to be humble before Him and before others.

The Lord also took me to Psalm 37:5-6, which says, "Commit your way to the Lord; trust in him, and he will do this: he will make your righteousness shine like the dawn, the justice of your cause like the noonday sun."

From this verse, I prayed that, yes, I want to be humble and act rightly in the eyes of others, but at the same time, I want God's opinion to matter more than anyone else's. I want to live for approval in God's eyes only. He is the one who will make my sincerity and righteousness before Him show through to others. I shouldn't try to impress people. If I impress God, He will take care of others' opinions.

> He who began a good work in you will carry it to completion until the day of Christ Jesus. (Philippians 1:6)

This verse comforts me in the knowledge that, even though I feel hopeless to change myself, it is God who will change me into the likeness of His Son, not me. Even though I feel like I've failed, it's okay; He will do the work in me.

Now here's the weird part: I didn't feel like I came to any sort of resolution through this. But after my quiet time, I was filled with an inexplicable inner joy throughout the rest of the day, which was odd.

I woke up to this message thinking, "Great, now my entire day is ruined. Why did it have to happen in the morning?" But that wasn't at all the case! I was so happy! And in retrospect, I know why. And here's my clincher for this devotional: **the conviction of the Holy Spirit *never* brings condemnation.**

He will never assault you with thoughts like "You're a terrible person! You're hopeless! You've blown it!" Those are only from the devil. When God convicts you, it is *always* constructive. He will build you up and leave you with encouragement, not hopelessness. So if you come away from a conversation with someone who has criticized you feeling broken down and discouraged, that is not from God. Reject it!

The person who criticized me left me feeling terrible about myself and hopeless about my situation. But when I took it to God, He left me with hope and joy. Yes, He convicted me and told me to change (with His help), which made my situation constructive, but I felt empowered when I closed my Bible. This is conviction from the Lord.

Go Deeper:

- What criticism have you allowed in your life from other people? Is it about you? Your walk with God? Your kids?

- Have you taken it to God? What does HE say about you? If you feel confused or discouraged, reject those thoughts. Condemnation is not from God. He is not the author of chaos, but of peace (I Corinthians 14:33). He did not come to condemn, but to save and redeem (John 3:17). Walk before Him as best you know how, not before men for their approval. Allow Him to convict you, yet embrace His encouragement, affirmation, and love, and let HIS description of you define you, not the judgment and accusations of others.

What's Next?

Pick a night this week during dinner to go around the table and share three things you love about each family member. Remember to remind yourself and your family what's great about you!

journal

> " For who is greater, the one who is at the table or the one who serves?
> Is it not the one who is at the table? But I am among you as one who serves. "
>
> ~ Luke 22:27

For Who Is Greater?

By: Samantha Swanson

The world has this idea that service is degrading. No one wants to do the dirty work, yet someone must step up. As a mom, it probably feels like this work is placed on you alone...day after day after day.

The good news is, you're not alone.

Jesus lived a life worth copying in every regard. He came not to be served, but to serve. Jesus did not ask for His disciples to wait on Him. Instead, He asked *them* to sit as He willingly washed their feet.

That sacrificial serving that you do every day? Jesus understands. (He did it too).

You probably agree that being a mom means doing the dirty work. It means waking up early and going to bed late. It means soiled laundry, lots of dishes, and greasy hair. Motherhood means feeling like you have reached the breaking point, but still choosing to love your children and husband one day at a time.

Growing up, I did not always appreciate how much my mom served in our household. She did the dirty work, and she did not complain. Only now, recently having moved away, do I see how hard she worked—often with little reward.

Of course, service and sacrifice within motherhood look a bit different. Though you are serving in many ways, that does not mean you should feel sorry for assigning chores or holding your kids accountable to responsibilities.

But here's the point: Though it is hard to serve with a good attitude, it is one of the best ways for you to connect with your kids and show them what it looks like to imitate Christ.

If you feel like your cheerful service is going unnoticed or unappreciated, know that you are following in your Savior's footsteps. *He* notices that you are doing *exactly* what you are called to do.

Go Deeper:

- How do you react to the word "service"—positively or negatively? How do you think you can best serve your family?

What's Next?

You are the hands and feet of Jesus, even when you feel like your work is small or unimportant, as you make dinner for your family at 8 o'clock at night or take the time to sit and listen to your daughter, sharing advice after she replays the story of her drama-filled day. Your service will help you connect with your children.

Remember that Jesus understands how difficult it is to serve faithfully—and with the right attitude. But also know that because He has done it before you, He knows exactly how to help you through as well.

Week Six ~ Day Three

Week Six

Also, don't forget to take some time away for yourself. Read a book for a few minutes, take a hot bath, or grab a quick coffee with a friend. You cannot be expected to continually pour into your family without ever taking time to refresh. Jesus went off to be alone in prayer—you need that time too.

Journal

> " Are you tired? Worn out? Burned out on religion? Come to me.
> Get away with me, and you'll recover your life. I'll show you how to take a real rest.
> Walk with me and work with me—watch how I do it. Learn the unforced
> rhythms of grace. I won't lay anything heavy or ill-fitting on you. "
> Keep company with me, and you'll learn to live freely and lightly.
>
> ~ Matthew 11:28-30 (MSG)

Desperate for Jesus

By: Brynne Gluch

Real life confession: I have spent a good part of my day procrastinating—doing low-priority chores, watching cute puppy videos, and drinking too much coffee. I know my soul is tired and desperate for Jesus because my body is telling me to find comfort at any cost.

My husband is a business owner, and this past weekend, we hosted a retreat for his company. We had been praying for months that the love of Jesus would be made known through our intentional preparation. It was an incredible time together. God moved powerfully in our hearts, bonding us toward our mission as a team.

But, this week of re-entry into family life has been brutal. We have been feeling the pressure of reconnecting with our kids, making holiday plans with out-of-town relatives, catching up with work, and moving into a new home (to name a few stresses). Our patience with each other has been thin as paper. On top of all that, my three-year-old daughter grabbed a pan off the stove while I was making dinner last night. I tried to pull it from her, but it was too late. As soon as we got her bandaged up, I collapsed into sobs on the kitchen floor.

This morning, I spoke with a treasured friend and mentor. She reminded me that last weekend was a big deal and that my soul must be tired. She reassured me that it was just an accident and that God is the healer. She encouraged me to shore up the strength of my heart with the Lord. So, I worked hard to get my kids to nap at the same time and then sang this song, "Lord I Need You" by Matt Maher, with my eyes closed:

> Without You, I fall apart
> You're the One that guides my heart
> Lord, I need You…Every hour I need You
> My one defense, my righteousness
> Oh God, how I need You.

And it was like my spirit woke up. Sister, if your body is weary, if your flesh is weak and falling to the temptation of false comforts, maybe your soul just needs to be with Jesus.

Go Deeper:

· Read all of Matthew Chapter 11. Allow the Word to wash over you and fill up your soul as you read. Seek to understand the cultural context, the writer's point of view, and the audience. Ask the Holy Spirit for revelation.

What's Next?

Is your body reminding your soul to be nourished by God's love? Challenge yourself to get daily, consistent time with God this week. Pray, sing, dance, or go for a walk. Keep a dream journal. Get creative! Alone time with God is not a one-size-fits-all relationship, but we are all dependent on His love!

Journal

_____

_____

_____

_____

_____

_____

_____

_____

_____

_____

_____

_____

_____

_____

_____

_____

_____

_____

_____

_____

_____

Week Six

Summer of Staying

~ Week Seven ~

"Blessed is the one who does not walk in step with the wicked or stand in the way that sinners take or sit in the company of mockers, but whose delight is in the law of the Lord, and who meditates on his law day and night. That person is like a tree planted by streams of water, which yields its fruit in season and whose leaf does not wither—whatever they do prospers." (Psalm 1:1-3)

My Dear Sister,

Recently, the Lord reminded me of a prayer I prayed when I was young. Long before I was married or had children, I read Psalm 1 and prayed that I would be "like a tree planted by streams of water, which yields its fruit in season, and whose leaf does not wither." At the time, I was just a young sapling, one of those trees just a few inches in diameter that was blown and tossed by the wind. I was imagining myself growing old there on the bank of the river, becoming a grandmother who had stood the test of time, who was so strong and wise, stable and steady.

This summer, it is our prayer that we become wise women who stay. How do we become women who are steady and stable, who stay engaged in relationships with their husbands and children? The answer is found in Psalm 1:2. We are to delight in the law of the Lord and meditate on it day and night. A tree planted by streams of water drinks deeply and never thirsts. Jesus says in John 4:14, "Whoever drinks the water I give them will never thirst. Indeed, the water I give them will become in them a spring of water welling up to eternal life." Wherever you go, whatever you face, make spending time in God's Word your priority. It is never too late to plant yourself by the Stream of Living Water.

Blessings and love,
Jennifer Valdois and the Help Club for Moms Team

"It is done. I am the Alpha and the Omega, the Beginning and the End.
To the thirsty I will give water without cost from the spring of the water of life.
Those who are victorious will inherit all this,
and I will be their God and they will be my children."

~ Jesus (Revelation 21:6-7)

Mom Tips

By: Leslie Leonard

"Above all, keep loving one another earnestly, since love covers a multitude of sins." ~ 1 Peter 4:8 (ESV)

The Wise Woman Builds Her Spirit:

- Watch/listen to a Help Club for Moms video located on our Facebook page while you do a load of laundry.
- Read your Bible aloud for 10 minutes every day this week, no matter where you are in your reading plan.

The Wise Woman Loves Her Husband:

- Meet your husband for lunch during the work week. Try to make this an adults-only lunch, and eat somewhere that he loves. Come mentally prepared with a few topics so you don't end up talking about the children.
- Pray aloud with your husband before bed at least once this week. If your husband is reluctant to pray aloud with you, then pray that God would open His heart and make him open to praying aloud with you on a regular basis.

The Wise Woman Loves Her Children:

- Declare a "no-work" day and let each child pick a fun activity for the family to do together.
- Read aloud to your children this week. Pick favorite books/Bible stories and gather together. Have each child tell the family what story they picked and why.

The Wise Woman Cares For Her Home:

- Deep clean the room you spend the most time in every day. For me, it's our family room. Declutter the shelves and tables. Dust all surfaces. Vacuum all areas and clean the windows. If necessary, clean the carpets.
- It's summer, so it is a perfect time to have a yard sale. Clean out all your closets and take out all the clothes or items that are too small, no longer worn, or have been sitting unused for longer than 6 months. Advertise in your neighborhood or online, and get rid of the clutter in your home. A clutter-free home makes for a clear mind.

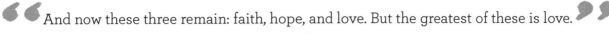

> "And now these three remain: faith, hope, and love. But the greatest of these is love."
>
> ~ 1 Corinthians 13:13

Leaving a Legacy of Love

By: Tara Davis

My dear friend, I know you try so hard to be the mom your kids need, the one God has called you to be. Between the messes, squabbles, and crazy life, maybe your fire and passion for this journey flickers a bit. Mine does too. Our time on this earth is so short, only just a vapor (James 4:14). And our time raising these precious little ones is even more fleeting. Oh, how I want my children to remember seeing Christ in me! A wise woman once told me to begin with the end in mind. Sisters, we must make a plan for the legacy we want to leave and stay the course as we allow God to make us into the women He desires us to be!

Have you merely been riding the waves of motherhood? Sweet sister, it is not too late to be intentional about writing your story and allowing Christ to write His story through you! Psalm 90:12 petitions the Lord, "Teach us to number our days, that we may gain a heart of wisdom." Who do you want to be during your remaining days? Begin walking more intentionally in God's calling for you! Let Christ transform you into the hands and feet of His love! He will make you into the kind, patient, faithful woman you long to be if you simply choose to surrender yourself and be renewed in Him.

When you intentionally walk with Him, He will shine through you, illuminating the darkness around you (2 Corinthians 4:6-7). As a daughter of the King, it is no longer you who lives, but Christ who lives in you (Galatians 2:20)! Begin walking in that today! Your children will see your faithfulness to Jesus and that will become the scaffolding they build their own lives upon!

The legacy we leave is our offering to the Lord that continues on long past our last breath on earth. Are you choosing to love today, my friend? Are you showing your children mercy and kindness? Are you personifying the character of Christ? Let us love with the purpose and selflessness written about in 1 Corinthians 13. This is the summer to submit your life to the Lord and allow Him to leave a legacy of love through you!

Go Deeper:

- Choose carefully who you follow. When you model your life after the whims of society, the things you view as important will hold no eternal value. Spend your time on this earth wisely as you model your life after God's Word. Evaluate where you stand today and make note in your journal of where you would like to be. How would you like to be remembered?

What's Next?

Pray for wisdom to discern the woman God has called you to be, and ask Him to lead you in becoming that woman. The next step is writing your mission statement. This does not have to be super formal, just a description of the legacy you want to begin living. Do you want to be known as a woman who exemplifies Christ's love, kindness, gentleness, forgiveness, and patience? Today is the day to begin the journey toward leaving a legacy of faithfulness!

journal

Week Seven

> " But I do not account my life of any value nor as precious to myself,
> if only I may finish my course and the ministry that I received
> from the Lord Jesus, to testify to the gospel of the grace of God. "
>
> ~ Acts 20:24 (ESV)

A Wise Woman Stays the Course

By: Jennifer Kindle

One day, when I was fed up with my young adult child, tempted to throw in the towel and let the chips fall where they may, my husband sweetly encouraged me, saying, "You have to finish this race strong with him, you can't give up now."

I wanted to give up. The finish line felt so far out of reach. The seeds I had sown seemed to have fallen on rocky ground. I was exhausted and tired of always redirecting this strong-willed child. My flesh wanted to leave him on his own to figure it out, and in all honesty, my flesh hoped he would fail and realize how much guidance he actually needed.

Like always, when I fall off the God-designed motherhood course, the relentless love and grace of Jesus swoops in and reminds me of truth, and He graciously guides me back on track. It's a tug-of-war between my flesh and what is honorable and noble. It's a fight to surrender on my end, but a beautiful grace offering on the Lord's.

A wise woman stays fixed on the heart of God. She stays in the Word so she can be quick to recognize lies disguised as truth. She stays in fellowship with her husband so she can eagerly accept his encouragement, and rebuke. She stays moving toward her children because she knows it's the heart of the Father to move toward His children.

A wise woman models the sacrificial love of Jesus by dying to herself so her children can reach their full potential. She knows her course is to wisely build into the hearts of her children. She trusts that by testifying and modeling the gospel of the grace of God before her children, they too will grow to be men and women who stay the course, move toward people, and finish strong the ministry set before them.

Go Deeper:
· Take time to ask the Lord for eyes to see the potential in your children, to see them as God does. As we begin seeing our children as the Lord does, we can eagerly choose to die to ourselves so they can reach their full potential.

What's Next?
Be a mom who makes the first move toward your children. Even when you are tempted to get away from them, make a move toward them, asking God for strength to humble yourself. A wise woman stays the course.

Week Seven ~ Day Two

Week Seven

journal

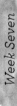

Week Seven

The Wise Woman Stays, Friends

By: Rae-Ellen Sanders

Good morning, friend! Time for your favorite beverage and time with your favorite person—Jesus! As you quiet your spirit, take a few minutes to consider Jesus as your best friend. Write in your journal what you think a perfect friend would look like. Kind, loyal, humble, patient, caring, a good listener, and fun to be around are a few from my list.

God's Word has a lot to say about friendship. There are many stories throughout Scripture about friends, their ups and downs, and their reconciliation. In fact, the disciple writers tell us how much Jesus prioritized relationships. Christ himself was a true friend to His disciples and others (Mary, Martha, Lazarus). Jesus Himself calls *us* friends! John 15:14 (NKJV) says, "You are my friends if you do whatever I command you." John 15:15 (NKJV) states, "No longer do I call you servants, for a servant does not know what his master is doing; but I have called you friends, for all things that I heard from my Father I have made known to you."

There are many beautiful friends in the Scriptures! Three of my favorites are Moses, Aaron, and Hur in Exodus 17:12. As long as Moses' arm was outstretched, the Israelites were undefeated; but when he was weary and his arm faltered, the army would lose. Both Aaron and Hur held up Moses' arms in his exhaustion. As true friends, they saw his need and stood on either side of him, sacrificing their own strength to see him succeed. My other favorite friendship story is of the paralyzed man in Mark 2:4 and again in Luke 5:19. The four friends passionately pushed through the crowds (while carrying their friend on the mat), and then diligently climbed on top of the roof (that must have been a sight to see). Once there, they dug a hole big enough to lower their invalid friend through the ceiling. I am sure this wasn't an easy task! Did they have spades in their back pockets? Did they fear ridicule from the Pharisees? They labored in compassionate unity just so their friend could be healed by Jesus! Can you imagine the exhilaration they must have felt watching their friend's legs restored? I am sure they found the sacrifice of their exerted energy was well worth the reward to see Jesus perform this miracle!

There is one more friendship story that I believe is truly amazing, and it ministers to my heart deeply—Jesus and the disciple Peter. Peter is known as the rock; he wholeheartedly believed in Jesus, even to the point of asking Jesus to wash all of him when Jesus washed the disciples' feet. He was the disciple who stepped out of the boat and walked on water! We are talking about a faithful and radical follower. At a fearful and unimaginable time, right after Jesus had been beaten and before His crucifixion, Peter denied knowing Jesus. The beautiful part of their reconciliation is that Jesus lovingly forgave Peter without condition. There weren't months of neglect or shunning. There was no backstabbing or gossip or even an argument. Jesus just asked Peter if He loved him, and when Peter said yes, Jesus forgave him and reassured Peter of his calling to love the Lord's sheep. I love this story because it's my story, and yours too! God is love, and even when we make mistakes, He readily forgives us if we repent. In Ephesians 4:32 (NKJV), God's Word instructs us to forgive: "And be kind to one another, tenderhearted, forgiving one another, even as God in Christ forgave you."

Week Seven

Go Deeper:

• Do you love like these friends in the Bible? Ask the Lord about going deeper with your friendships by loving their children, praying for their marriages, and forgiving any offenses. Ask the Lord to help you lend a listening ear more often, receiving the gift of just sitting and being there with your friends. Perhaps you need to extend love to a friend through kindness, or maybe you need to go the extra mile by making a meal or lending a hand with childcare. Ask the Lord to help you be more sensitive to the needs of your friends and to treasure and treat your friends as the gifts they are!

What's Next?

Are *you* friends with Jesus? Do you spend time with Him and share your deepest secrets with Him? He died on the cross for your sins so you can have eternal life with Him. If you receive this free gift of grace, follow and obey like the disciples did. Seek righteousness and peace, and Jesus will be your friend too! Nurture your relationship with Jesus by meeting with Him daily. Talk to Him, write notes to Him, and give gifts of service to Him. Be loyal, sit with Him, and mourn with Him. Tune your ears to listen to Him. Rejoice, be merry, and fall in love with Him! Tell your children that Jesus is their friend too and that they can talk to Him anytime! Point out good character when you see it, and use every opportunity to talk about how great the Father's love is for us!

> Greater love has no one than this, than to lay down one's life for his friends. (John 15:13 NKJV)

Journal

> " Therefore, my beloved brothers, be steadfast, immovable, always abounding in the work of the Lord, knowing that in the Lord your labor is not in vain. "
>
> ~ 1 Corinthians 15:58 (ESV)

But I Just Need to Get Away!

By: Katie Sadler

The van was calling my name. The walls of my house were closing in and my to-do list was continually lengthening...not shortening. I just wanted to run away from it all.

Have you ever felt like this? If you could jump in the car and go...you could escape the heaviness of what is staring you in the face: the crying littles, the laundry, the mouthy teenager, the loud music, the demands of wifehood, the endless job of cooking, and even the after-hour pressures from the workplace.

A wise woman stays.

Staying is hard sometimes, but Scripture tells us that, when we are steadfast, when we stay and make efforts as unto the Lord, our labor is not in vain! It doesn't just benefit *us*. Our tired feet and backs yield fruit, beautiful fruit. The days we want to run, but instead stay and follow through, they yield fruit.

Staying is a discipline. It is a way of life that we can train in ourselves. If we have a tendency to run (by physically leaving or checking out mentally) when the going gets tough, God gives us the ability to stay.

Hebrews 12:11 (ESV) tells us, "For the moment all discipline seems painful rather than pleasant, but later it yields the peaceful fruit of righteousness to those who have been trained by it." Isn't that true? Staying isn't always the pleasant choice, but it's the fruitful choice. It's the choice that gives our children a sense of safety, knowing we are here when they cry. It's the choice that tells our husbands we are devoted, even when it is hard. Staying tells our teenagers we are for them, even when we don't see eye to eye and they are making bad choices.

Staying, steadfastness, doing it all because we love Jesus, makes it all worthwhile.

Go Deeper:

- If you know you're a runner but you want to be steadfast and stay, ask the Lord to give you the courage to do so. If life is often overwhelming you, make sure you haven't taken on too many extra burdens. Start by looking at your calendar. Look to see if you can let just one thing go. Maybe you can say no to the extra playdate this week, or the favor a friend asked of you. "No" is scary sometimes, but sometimes it is the right kind of scary.

What's Next?

This week, maybe you need to carve out intentional time to rest, refresh, and revive your reason for staying. Take a walk, a bath, or even go somewhere, but do it intentionally and not with a heart of running. Remember that your goal is steadfastness that yields fruit—a strong marriage, healthy children, and even trustworthiness as an employee. Remember that God's Word is full of encouragement for the weary. God can and will give you courage and strength. Rest in Him by reading His Word and talking to Him in prayer; and He will answer you, providing you with joy and strength in motherhood, wifehood, and all the other hats you wear.

journal

Food for the Soul

For many people, summer means grilling. We love to grill year-round, but especially in the summer. One year, I was looking for a grilling recipe that was an alternative to just grilling a big hunk of meat. I came across this recipe in a magazine. Over the years, our family has adapted the original recipe to our liking, and it is now one of our go-to summer recipe favorites. It combines great summer vegetables like zucchini and yellow squash with a burst of flavor from salsa verde.

This recipe is a nice, healthy, light meal, and since the grill is being used for most of the cooking, it's also fast and easy, with minimal cleanup. Serve it alongside your favorite Mexican side dish, like chips and dip, or even a fresh salad. You can adapt this recipe to cook on the stove top if you don't have a grill. This recipe does make a lot, so it can be halved for a smaller family. It feeds my family of 7, and we still have leftovers!

SUMMER VEGGIE TOSTADAS By: Brandi Carson

Ingredients:

2-3 medium chicken breasts, butterflied open

2-3 medium yellow squash, quartered lengthwise

2-3 medium zucchini, quartered lengthwise

1 large red onion sliced into ⅓ inch rings, make sure rings don't separate

1 bag of frozen corn, heated according to directions on the package

8-10 soft taco-size tortillas

8-ounce bag of shredded Mexican-blend cheese

canola spray

olive oil

½-1 teaspoon cumin

salt and pepper to taste

salsa verde

Directions:

1. Preheat grill to medium-high heat. While grill is preheating, coat butterflied chicken with olive oil and season both sides with cumin, adding salt and pepper to taste. Set aside.

2. In a separate dish, season the zucchini, yellow squash, and red onion with oil, salt, and pepper. Try to keep onion ring slices together for easier grilling.

3. Place chicken breast on one side of the grill and vegetables on the other side. The chicken will need 4-6 minutes on each side, which will create nice charred grill marks. Watch carefully and don't overcook. Remove from grill when done and let rest for 5-10 minutes before dicing.

4. Vegetables will need 3-6 minutes on each side. They will have nice grill marks on each side. The red onions might need a little longer, maybe 5-7 minutes on each side. Make sure they are cooked enough in the middle to get rid of that raw onion flavor and to sweeten them up a bit. The onions do okay with a little extra char on them. When vegetables are done, remove from grill and set aside until cool enough to handle. Remember to turn off your grill.

5. Dice chicken and vegetables into small pieces and mix together in a bowl. Season as needed. Mix in the corn and set bowl aside.

SUMMER VEGGIE TOSTADAS

(Directions Continued):

6. Once tostada filling is done, preheat oven to broil. Take the number of tortillas needed and stab each one with a fork several times. This helps prevent the tortillas from bubbling up when they are being broiled. Spray tortillas on each side and place on a sheet pan to broil. You may need several batches, depending on the size of the tortillas and how many total tostadas you are making. Broil tortilla until golden brown, then flip. Repeat. Broil until the other side is golden brown as well. Watch tortillas and try to pop any large bubbles that may begin to form. This helps to maintain an even surface for your veggie mixture.

7. Remove tortillas from oven and let cool slightly until firm. Add enough veggie mixture on top of the tortilla to form a single layer, not mounding it too much. Top with cheese and broil again until cheese is melted and bubbly. Remove from oven.

8. Top with the desired amount of salsa verde, and slice like a pizza or eat whole.

To cook on stove top instead of grill, you will simple sauté the chicken first, and then set it aside. Dice up veggies into small pieces first and sauté on medium-high heat until cooked. Dice chicken and add it to the corn and veggies. Season to taste. Then follow step 6 on.

Summer of Staying
~ Week Eight ~

Hello Sweet Mama!

Can you hear that sound? It's the roar of school revving up again. School shopping, carpools, lunches, and no more time at the lake. A subtle stressfulness settles in our stomachs. We wonder, "Are we ready to handle fall and everything that comes with it?"

Undoubtedly, letting go of summer is a trying transition, but even so, I challenge you to join me in unveiling the joy around us. Did you know that all the latest research on happiness suggests that joy comes from having a grateful heart?

Perhaps you are gigantically grateful for school to start and routines to get back to normal. Now, even more importantly, look high and low for ways to be appreciative of your children and your role as a mom. Your baby is soft, warm, and loves to be in your arms. Your boy is growing like a weed and will never be this small again. Your girl has such a gentle, tender heart. Embrace these good times and thank God for the little loved ones around you. Savor your moments with them because they are passing so quickly!

Psalm 90 reminds us to number our days, and Psalm 127 says that our children are arrows in our quivers and gifts from God. Thankfulness for the precious people around us is what cultivates joy in our hearts and helps us to be the gentle, connected mamas that stay richly engaged and love well, even as summertime wanes and school beckons.

May you have a bountiful and blessed fall!

Love and Blessings,
Kristi Valentine and the Help Club for Moms Team

> **I don't have to chase extraordinary moments to find happiness—it's right in front of me if I'm paying attention and practicing gratitude.**
>
> ~ Brené Brown

Mom Tips

By: Leslie Leonard

"A man without self-control is like a city broken into and left without walls." ~ Proverbs 25:28 (ESV)

The Wise Woman Builds Her Spirit:

- Connect with your prayer partner this week. Make it a priority and keep the call to 10 minutes. Set a timer if you need the reminder.
- Write 1 Peter 5:7-10 on your notecards or record it on your phone. Take the time to memorize the verses by the end of the week. Journal about what the verses mean to you.

The Wise Woman Loves Her Husband:

- Take to the kitchen and learn to cook something new with your spouse this week. Find a recipe that appeals to your family and stretches your skills. Grow closer as you hone your knife skills and spice up more than the food.
- Text your husband and tell him what a wonderful partner he is. Be specific about something in the last week that made you happy that you married him.

The Wise Woman Loves Her Children:

- Head to the local ice cream parlor after dinner. (Bonus if it's close enough to walk or ride bikes).
- Pray for your children's friendships this week. Summer is filled with friends coming and going. Pray that friends are kind and love your children for who God created them to be.

The Wise Woman Cares For Her Home:

- Wash all the windows in your home both inside and outside. Clean the window sills and tracks too.
- Take a break from the Internet. Do Facebook, Pinterest, or Instagram cause you to neglect your housework or family? Maybe it's time to turn off your computer or smartphone and spend that time with people who love you the most.

> " My son, do not forget my teaching, but keep my commands in your heart, for they will prolong your life many years and bring you peace and prosperity. "

~ Proverbs 3:1-2

Real Men in the Making

By: Mari Jo Mast

Raising boys makes a mama dig deep! My husband and I are still raising three. Our oldest son is now married and is raising two of his own. A while ago, my husband and I had a Holy Spirit-inspired conversation (unplanned) with one of our teen sons about what it means to be a man. We talked about responsibility, conflict resolution, accountability, humility, leadership, chores, obedience, etc. All the things a man should strive to be—all the important things. But we discovered that in the end, it really boils down to one thing: a boy becomes a real man when he consistently hears the voice of God and obeys. That is all.

I freely shared with our son, "A mama can rest when she knows her son obeys the Holy Spirit. It puts her heart at ease because she has nothing to fear or worry about."

My husband and I consistently speak life over our sons. We express our belief in the Holy Spirit's active work in their lives and affirm that they hear His voice. We encourage them to always obey.

How do young boys begin to hear and obey God? Honestly, it's far easier caught than taught. It begins by hearing and obeying us as parents first. It continues as we parents fellowship with, and listen to, the Holy Spirit ourselves. Our boys are watching our everyday walk with Jesus. How we live teaches and helps mold their own opinion about who He is. As we trust Him, so will they. As we love, so will they. As we obey, so will they.

Truly, God defines manhood like no one else can. He covers *all* the bases in His Word and those truths bring a balance we can trust and surrender to. I believe that as we parent from this place of deep devotion to Jesus (listening and obeying), our children will naturally follow. In that process, we raise up the next generation of men for His Kingdom!

So, take heart as you raise those rough and tumble boys, sweet mom! Though they may not act the part, deep down inside they are tender and soft, wanting to become real men. Remember to show them the way even if you feel they're not paying attention. I dare say they are much more aware than we give them credit for. With Jesus, you have what it takes!

Go Deeper:
- Be aware of the presence of Jesus as you raise your sons for His glory. You can't ever spend too much time with Him. He is always with you, helping you be a godly example to your sons! You can always read His Word and pray if you need answers.

What's Next?
My husband is taking our sons out into the mountains to shoot today. He has found it's a great way to connect with them. Encourage your husband in a positive way (not nagging) to take your son/sons out on a date just to spend some quality time together. Even if they don't talk much, just hanging out brings positive

results! You could even set it up for them to make it easier. Depending on your son's age, below are some great ideas:

1. Go shooting at a local gun range (a favorite for our boys).
2. Hang out at Buffalo Wild Wings and watch a football game (also a favorite).
3. If you have a membership at a gym, work out together.
4. Go fishing (make sure you have a license, if needed).
5. Hike a mountain together.
6. Go camping for a night. Help them pack and prepare.
7. Work on a simple project together.
8. Go bicycling.
9. Cook a meal together. Have them choose the menu; you can buy the ingredients.
10. Play with remote controlled vehicles.
11. Go to a local go-kart racetrack.

Journal

_____
_____
_____
_____
_____
_____
_____
_____
_____
_____
_____
_____
_____
_____
_____

> **" "** We love Him, because He first loved us. **" "**
> ~ 1 John 4:19 (KJV)

We Just Do

By: Daphne Close

I called my daughter over to me and had her sit on my lap. (Let me tell you how thankful I am that this one daughter of mine still fits!) We cuddled for a few minutes, and then out of curiosity I asked her, "Why do you love me?"

"I just do," she replied.

These three short words may not mean a lot at face value, but they immediately led me to an absolute truth about God:

> We love Him because He first loved us. (1 John 1:19 KJV)

I learned this verse years ago, but God's Living Word struck me in a new and profound way when my daughter said those words. Why does my daughter love me? It's because I first loved her. From the example of love I have shown, she has learned it, felt it, embraced it, and then reciprocated. What we have together is a beautiful gift.

But then I wondered, why do I love her? Why do I love anyone at all? Plain and simple, it's because God first loved me.

Sometimes, we love others because they do things for us, but that's just conditional love. When you truly love someone, you can't provide a rational explanation. You just do. Remember, dear mama, you learned this kind of love from only one person: your Heavenly Father. And that is also a beautiful gift—the *most* precious gift of all.

Our love toward the Lord should not be based on feelings. In Matthew 22:37, Jesus says that we are to "love the Lord your God with all your heart, and with all your mind, and with all your soul." We are told, commanded really, to love God!

1 John 4:8 and 16 both declare that "God is love." He's so full of love that He desired to pour His love into others. Thus, He created the universe, all living creatures, non-living objects, and finally, us. To this very day, He continues to create so that He can continue to love, love, love, love, love.

We may not be able to fathom completely why He loves us; sometimes we even feel unlovable and undeserving of His perfect love. But, through all of that, we love Him. It is in our hearts, and we just do.

Go Deeper:

- Read 1 John 4:7-21. Read it slowly, intentionally, whispering the passage out loud so that it sinks into your heart.

What's Next?

Set a reminder to read 1 Corinthians 13:4-8 (the Love Chapter) out loud daily. Don't just read it to yourself; read it with your husband and your children. In particular, read it when tension stirs up within the family!

Week Eight

Journal

_____
_____
_____
_____
_____
_____
_____
_____
_____
_____
_____
_____
_____
_____
_____
_____
_____
_____
_____
_____
_____
_____
_____
_____
_____

Week Eight ~ Day Two   ~ 96 ~

> " When Jesus saw her weeping, and the Jews who had come along
> with her also weeping, he was deeply moved in spirit and troubled.
> 'Where have you laid him?' he asked. 'Come and see, Lord,' they replied. Jesus wept. "
>
> ~ John 11:33-35

From a Daughter's Perspective: Do You Know What Your Love Does?

By: Elise Turner

Mom and dad, you will never know the power of your love.

Today, when I got home from school, I dropped my backpack and wept. The night before, I knelt on my bed to pray, and I cried to God for two hours. I asked Him to speak, hoping maybe He would be able to explain my sadness. I heard nothing.

I'm a 20-year-old college student living in a townhome 30 minutes away from my parents. When I'm overcome with any emotion, the first thing I do is call my mom. She shares them with me, the happy moments and the not-so-happy moments. I called her today, a weeping wreck. And because my dad happened to be five minutes away from my house, he came to save me, my knight in a shining GMC Envoy. I talked to him through sobs and sniffles:

"Dad, I don't know what's wrong. All I know is that I can't stop crying. And I can't hear God. And I don't feel Him close to me."

Noticing that I had blown through the sopping tissue in my hand, he pulled a white silk handkerchief from the pocket of the driver's side door.

"Where in the world did you get this?" I asked the man who is content to blow his nose with a McDonald's napkin.

Probably wishing I hadn't asked, he responded, "Elise, it was the weirdest thing. A strange old lady came up to me the other day at my cousin's funeral and handed it to me. She looked me dead in the eye and said, 'Here, this is for you.' But I wasn't even crying. And I keep seeing it here thinking I need to throw it away, but for some reason I don't."

Dad, I believe with all my heart that God made you keep that handkerchief for me. See, He made it easy for you to love me that day, and He equipped you with everything you would need to comfort me. He had a forethought: that His daughter would be sad on some dreadful Monday, and she would need to know that Jesus is close.

Through the love of my father, I have learned so much about my Abba and my Jesus. I grew up shielded by love and the security it provides. In my yellow gingerbread home, I was free to imagine and dream. I never second-guessed the love of my father. I don't know where I would be without the prayers of my parents.

Today, my father taught me that Jesus is close to the brokenhearted (Psalm 34:18). Jesus wept with me, just like He wept with Mary and Martha when their brother died. He did not cry because Lazarus' life was irretrievable: He knew Lazarus would live again. He cried because His daughters' hearts were broken, and He could not bear to see them sad. Jesus feels everything we feel. When we are "brought down to the dust; our bodies [clinging] to the ground" (Psalm 44:25), Jesus doesn't just snap His fingers and make everything better again. He does something that speaks much more to His character. He meets us in the dirt, gives up His place on high to be with the lowly, the broken-spirited. More than that, He gives us hope, "And hope does not put us to shame, because God's love has been poured out into our hearts through the Holy Spirit..." (Romans 5:5).

Mom, thank you for always answering.

Dad, thank you for following the lead of the Holy Spirit.

Your love makes me strong.

Go Deeper:

• Pray to understand the love of the Father. This is a love that is always present, that is the ultimate expression of empathy. And mommas, know that the best thing you can do for your children is to show them this love.

What's Next?

Next time your children are sad, remind them that Jesus sees them in their sadness and that His heart breaks for them. There is a purpose, even for sadness, and that is to draw us closer to God and closer to our loved ones. Make your children a warm cup of tea, watch their favorite show with them, and know that, in these times, God will speak through your love more than your words.

journal

_____

_____

_____

_____

_____

_____

_____

_____

_____

_____

_____

> " Set your minds on things above, not on earthly things. "
>
> ~ Colossians 3:2

Above the Storm

By: Tara Fox

One day while my children were bickering, God told me, "Be above the storm." I was getting too emotionally involved in their arguments, so I was unable to remain calm and rational. He showed me a storm raging in the clouds above the earth. My view was like an astronaut seeing a storm from way above. Even though we are near the storms in which our children are involved, it doesn't mean we have to become part of the storm emotionally. Sometimes, we need a reminder to step back and detach our feelings from what is going on so we are able to respond to them appropriately instead of reacting based on feelings. This has been one of the most difficult things for me as a parent, but God continues to give me wisdom each day on how to deal with situations as they arise.

I wish I could have more of the Jesus effect when I say, "Quiet, be still," and my children would stop like the storm on the sea! Even though it doesn't quite happen that way in our houses, we can look to Jesus for ways to handle each storm that comes our way.

Here are some lessons we learn from reading about Jesus calming the storm in Mark 4:

- Even Jesus needed a break from His work and ministry. Mark 4:36 tells us that he left the crowd behind. Make sure you get time away from people to rest and refuel with God. It is essential to keeping your peace in the storms that your family will encounter. If you are faithful to consistently meet with Jesus, He will calm your heart and renew your mission.

- Jesus was not surprised when the storm arose. In fact, He knew it was coming because he is all-knowing. We may not be all-knowing, but we can anticipate that problems will arise. When we plan for time in our days to train and discipline, we will expect the interruptions and not get as frustrated or angry when they happen.

- Jesus slept peacefully while the storm was raging. We can also rest peacefully at night knowing that God will take care of our children. He has it all under control. Sometimes, sleeplessness does happen, but remember that God made you to sleep.

- Jesus wanted the disciples to have faith even when the circumstances looked bleak. It is important to Him that we respond in Faith instead of fearing what may happen to our children or family. We can teach our children valuable life lessons in the midst of trial, bad choices, or mistakes by the way we handle things. Each storm is a learning opportunity for all. No matter what issues our children are facing, we must put our faith in Jesus and not in what we currently see or feel.

- Jesus responded in authority. He knew He had greater power than any storm. We too can respond in our authority in Jesus Christ through prayer, fasting, and faith, speaking over the storm as Jesus did. There is something about our spoken word that allows God to work, Satan to be put in his place, and ourselves to get in line with what God is already doing.

- Jesus went right back to ministering to others when He arrived on shore. In fact, that was His plan before He even arrived. Even though we need rest, God has given us the ability to continue to love and train our children day after day.

Heaven is my throne, and the earth is my footstool. (Isaiah 66:1)

Let's dwell with Him, above the storm.

Week Eight ~ Day Four

Go Deeper:

• Think about the things that set you off. Make a plan for how you will respond when these things occur. Oftentimes, I need to walk away and spend a few minutes in prayer until I can calm down.

What's Next?

What are the causes of the current storms in your children's lives?

Are you emotionally involved in the storms or are you able to "be above?" Pray and ask God to help you emotionally separate from the discord so that you are able to be like a refreshing summer rain in your children's lives.

journal

_____

_____

_____

_____

_____

_____

_____

_____

_____

_____

_____

_____

_____

_____

_____

_____

_____

_____

_____

Summer of Staying

~ Week Nine ~

Dearest Mom,

I am so thankful that you have been with us this summer. Being intentional and making time to spend with the Lord is the best gift you can give your husband as his wife, and your children as their mother. Nothing else in this world will equip you to persevere through the hard times like the Word of God and His Holy Spirit dwelling inside of you!

Summer sure is a glorious time, isn't it? The freedom and flexibility that the warm weather brings is a magical feeling. But every year, it has to end. We all want to enjoy each minute that this season has left, but alas, we have to start planning and preparing for what is imminent.

As mothers, we are always thinking about what is to come. What will the next school year bring? When will my toddler be potty-trained? When will my baby ever walk?! The beauty of these changes in motherhood is found in staying put and appreciating the moment, but also in accepting the change when it arrives.

Mamas, I would like to encourage you with these verses out of Ecclesiastes:

> For everything there is a season, and a time for every purpose under heaven: a time to be born, and a time to die; a time to plant, and a time to pluck up that which has been planted. (Ecclesiastes 3:1-2)

Pray for that kind of patience and perspective. Pray to grow and stay in your season. Pray to learn and endure through all things. You can do this, friend!

Love and Blessings,
Rachel Jones and the Help Club for Moms Team

> *Relying on God has to start all over every day,*
> *as if nothing has yet been done.*
>
> *~ C.S. Lewis*

Mom Tips

By: Leslie Leonard

"Let love be genuine. Abhor what is evil; hold fast to what is good. Love one another with brotherly affection. Outdo one another in showing honor." ~ Romans 12:9-10 (ESV)

The Wise Woman Builds Her Spirit:

- Continue to work on your Prayer Binder.
- Reach out and invite someone over for coffee who isn't in your close-knit circle of friends. Pray and ask God to show you who needs a friend or someone to talk to right now. Ask and He will answer.

The Wise Woman Loves Her Husband:

- Say "hello" to your husband and family as soon as you hear them walk into the house every day this week. Acknowledge them when they walk into a room. These little moments show our loved ones that they matter to us!
- Make your husband's favorite meal or dessert this week. Have it be a surprise on a particularly long or stressful workday.

The Wise Woman Loves Her Children:

- Have your children help give your pets a bath this week. Having pets is a big responsibility, and children should take an active role. Decide where to bathe the animals and gather the supplies. Let the children help lather, rinse, and dry the pets.
- Seek out new nature walks, state parks, or city parks and get outside with your children this week. While walking/hiking, teach your children Revelation 4:11, Psalm 139:14, Psalm 23:2-3, and Job 12:7-9.

The Wise Woman Cares For Her Home:

- Visit your local farmers' market for fresh produce and fruit. It's a great way to support local farmers and merchants; plus, it's a great family outing.
- Dust all the ceiling fans and chandelier light fixtures in your home.

> **"** For God has not given us a spirit of fear,
> but of power and of love and of a sound mind. **"**
>
> ~ 2 Timothy 1:7 (NKJV)

Worry, Worry, Worry: What Do You Worry About?

By: Deb Weakly

When my children were babies, I worried about them dying in their sleep.

When they were toddlers, I worried about them getting really sick or having a serious accident.

When they were in elementary school, I worried about my complete inadequacy as a mom and felt like I did not know how to raise my children to be Christians.

When they were in high school, I worried about them turning away from God or not following Him.

Worry, worry, worry.

What does it accomplish? Nothing! It causes sleepless nights and days filled with dread. Worry steals our joy and allows Satan to gain a foothold in our thoughts. In my life, my worry and anxiety got so bad that I got to the point of not enjoying my life and the family God had given me. When I focused on the bad things that could happen, I hardly noticed the good things right in front of me.

Jesus tells us specifically not to worry about tomorrow. I love the story that Corrie Ten Boom tells about how God gives you grace one day at a time. When someone asked her how she could have endured the persecution and suffering she went through in the German concentration camps during World War II, she said she had the unfathomable grace of God to help her.

She said when she was a little girl, she would travel on the trains with her dad quite frequently. He understood that she did not need her train ticket for their journey until right before she stepped onto the train. He gave her the ticket just at the time she needed it.

Corrie said that God's grace is like that train ticket. We don't get it until right when we need it. So, when we worry about tomorrow and all the things that could go wrong, we don't have God's grace to help us because we are not there yet. We stress and stress to no avail. It doesn't help, and in fact, worry only hurts us. We can't do anything about tomorrow anyway. So why not trust God for today and live in the moment?

> Therefore do not worry about tomorrow, for tomorrow will worry about itself. Each day has enough trouble of its own. (Matthew 6:34)

God has given us everything we need—His power in us, His word, and His grace one day at a time. He knows we want our kids to follow Him and love Him all the days of their lives. God knows we have financial, marital, or health issues. He is a good, good Father and will help us through whatever we may face!

Go Deeper:

- How about you? Do you worry? Be honest. Write what you worry about in your journal, then ask God to help you trust Him more, pray, and walk by faith. Find a Scripture that encourages you to trust God. For example, when my kids were little, I was worried that I had no idea how to have a Christian home and raise up kids who love God. I wrote Isaiah 42:16 on my bathroom mirror in dry-erase marker so I could focus on it every day:

  > I will lead the blind by ways they have not known, along unfamiliar paths I will guide them; I will turn the darkness into light before them and make the rough places smooth. These are the things I will do; I will not forsake them.

- That verse always brought me peace, helped me not to give up, and encouraged me to trust God to help me.

What's Next?

When my children were little, I used to have what I called a "Worry Box." During times of anxiety and worry, I took a moment and wrote down what I was worried about, put it in the box, and gave it to God. Every once in awhile, I would look back over all of the things I had written and was always amazed at what troubled me. I began to realize that the vast majority of stuff I worried about never came true. Now in my 50s, I find myself wanting to live by faith more and to encourage my family to do the same. Pray that you can live your life walking with God, trusting Him more, and worrying less.

journal

_____

_____

_____

_____

_____

_____

_____

_____

_____

_____

> " For I proclaim the name of the Lord: ascribe greatness to our God.
> He *is* the Rock, His work *is* perfect; for all His ways *are* justice,
> a God of truth and without injustice; righteous and upright *is* He. "
>
> ~ Deuteronomy 32:3-4 (NKJV)

Jesus is The Rock!

By: Rae-Ellen Sanders

Ah, summertime! How many of you have gone on cross-country road trips with your families to see the Grand Canyon or to Mount Rushmore? These rock formations and monuments are major tourist destinations that are created by amazing sculpting talent—the very hand of God. So many places around our world draw attention to big rocks: Stonehenge, Ayers Rock, Bryce Canyon, El Capitan, Fingal's Cave, Half Dome, Independence Rock, Balancing Rock (this one is in my hometown), and even Plymouth Rock, to name just a few.

These rocks are impressive! They are solid and can't be moved! God's Word repeatedly says that *He is the rock* and indeed there is none other. Grab your Bible and be prepared to look up and write down the following verses in your journal: 1 Samuel 2:2, 2 Samuel 22:2, 2 Samuel 22:32, 2 Samuel 22:47.

As wise women, we need to *stay* built up on the Rock. Meditating on the previous verses will fill you with wonder at our powerful Papa God. The parallel between rocks and our Heavenly Father can be found throughout Scripture. A word search for "rock" on Bible Gateway really opened my eyes to the significance of this title! Below you will find additional verses on God being the Rock:

Deuteronomy 32:18 – the one who begot you

Deuteronomy 32:37 – is your refuge

Judges 6:21 – a consuming fire

Psalm 18:2 – fortress, deliverer, stronghold

Psalm 27:5 – lifter of your soul

Psalm 31:2 – fortress of defense

Psalm 31:3 – leads and guides

Psalm 40:2 – sure foundation, establishes steps

Psalm 61:2 – comforter

Psalm 62:2 – your defense

Psalm 62:7 – salvation, glory, and strength

Psalm 71:1 – your trust

Psalm 71:3 – fortress

Psalm 78:35 – most high God, redeemer

Psalm 81:16 – satisfies

Psalm 89:26 – Father, God, salvation

Psalm 92:15 – upright, righteous

Psalm 94:22 – defense, refuge

Psalm 95:1 – salvation

Isaiah 17:10 – stronghold

Isaiah 28:16 – cornerstone, sure foundation

Isaiah 44:8 – no other!

Isaiah 48:21 – your provision

1 Corinthians 10:4 – the *rock is Christ!*

Go Deeper:

- After reading the verses listed above, I feel assured that my feet are firm when I stand on the Rock. What promises! What a great place of security!

- In Matthew 7:24-27 (NKJV) we read the words of Jesus: "Therefore whoever hears these sayings of Mine, and does them, I will liken him to a wise man who built his house on the rock: and the rain descended, the floods came, and the winds blew and beat on that house; and it did not fall, for it was founded on the rock. But

everyone who hears these sayings of Mine, and does not do them, will be like a foolish man who built his house on the sand: and the rain descended, the floods came, and the winds blew and beat on that house, and it fell. And great was its fall."

- Also in Luke 6:48 (NKJV), "He is like a man building a house, who dug deep and laid the foundation on the rock. And when the flood arose, the stream beat vehemently against that house, and could not shake it, for it was founded on the **rock**."

- Jesus is the *rock*! We are to build our lives on Him! We need to be wise and make every opportunity to stay grounded in His Word so that we will have a firm foundation on which to stand.

What's Next?

This is "heavy," huh? Sorry to be so punny. Take that road trip, and when in awe of God's creation, reflect on the Almighty Creator! Take a nature walk with your kids and talk about rocks and God's imageries. Homeschool moms, use geology to talk about how mighty God is and how He is all of the characteristics listed in Scripture. Next time you're at a lake, skip rocks and ponder the awesomeness of our God. Take the next few minutes to meditate on Psalm 31:1-4, and then end your time of Bible study with singing! I love the old hymn "The Solid Rock."

"The Solid Rock"

My hope is built on nothing less
Than Jesus' blood and righteousness;
I dare not trust the sweetest frame,
But wholly lean on Jesus' name.

Refrain:
On Christ, the solid rock, I stand—
All other ground is sinking sand,
All other ground is sinking sand.

When darkness veils His lovely face,
I rest on His unchanging grace;
In every high and stormy gale
My anchor holds within the veil.
<refrain>

His oath, His covenant, His blood
Support me in the whelming flood;
When all around my soul gives way,
He then is all my hope and stay.
<refrain>

When He shall come with trumpet sound,
Oh may I then in Him be found,
Dressed in His righteousness alone,
Faultless to stand before the throne.
<refrain>

Journal

_____

_____

_____

_____

_____

> " I will put my laws in their minds and write them on their hearts.
> I will be their God, and they will be my people.
> No longer will they teach their neighbor, or say to one another,
> 'Know the Lord,' because they will all know me, from the least of them to the greatest. "
>
> ~ Hebrews 8:10b-11

Raising Our Children in True Freedom

By: Mari Jo Mast

Learning to love my children like Jesus loves me has been a long journey—a journey I'm still walking. False ideas I carry about His character constantly come crashing down. Through the Scriptures and His Spirit, I learn who He really is: He is **love**, and that covers a lot of stuff, including mistakes and sin. I need to set aside my expectations and ideals in order to embrace His way. Things that are very important to me take a back seat, while what's true according to the Word now occupies the throne of my heart. You see, a mind directed by the flesh constantly disagrees with the character of the Spirit (read Romans 8:7). In the same way, our natural ideas about child training clash with the teachings of Jesus.

Parenting from our flesh comes so easily and naturally! We want perfect kids, so our mind exalts perfectionism. We like hard-core rules and punishment because they look like neat lines that make sense and keep our kids in check. Sadly, we often want to judge them rather than disciple and administer mercy. You see, if we have love deficits in our own hearts, the temptation of raising robot kids without love and relationship will pop up continually. This is not God's heart! It fails because outward pressure and containment don't actually bring lasting change in us or our children. The proof is in the pudding: what happens when the restrictions are removed?

If we are honest, what we desire most as a parent is for our kids to come to love Jesus and obey Him when we aren't around, right? At least that's what I desire as a mom. I want them to be clean from the inside out and to be self-governed so they will do the right thing even when the rules are gone. But how is that even possible?

There is no true hope beyond Jesus. He alone makes freedom attainable. His overcoming power is so much greater than our feeble restrictions and boundaries! Even when our children are young, it's our parental mandate to lead them to Him. Their "want to's" change when they are born of His Spirit because He miraculously writes His laws on their hearts. It's our job to nurture them in the teachings of Jesus, and it's the Holy Spirit's job to bring the freedom!

In John 8:31b-32, Jesus said, "If you hold to my teaching, you are really my disciples. Then you will know the truth, and the truth will set you free." How do we become disciples of Jesus? By obeying and living love—His way. Our children become His followers too as they experience Him through us. These teachings are definitely meant to be passed on to them. We shouldn't hypocritically hold our kids captive when God has provided a lasting remedy! It's good for us to re-evaluate our rules, ideas, and methods compared to our Lord's. Lest we forget, Jesus helped us out by reaching the perfect standard when He died as a spotless, sinless sacrifice. We should not expect one ounce more of our children than we expect of ourselves.

Mom, learn to give yourself grace. We freely give when we freely receive, and this is where it all begins.

It's okay to consult God before you deal with your child's bad attitude and to pray for His counsel before you react. The things He reveals when we ask are astounding and eye-opening, even though it may take time! Our own hands only provide a temporary fix, often keeping us from getting revelation from the Giver of *Life*. Removing our own ideas and trading them for God's truth brings answers. Grace (what He gives us on a daily basis) exposes what's in our hearts, simultaneously revealing our need for Him too. When He comes into the picture, into our story, we become empowered to live *above* sin. In fact, sin loses its tight grip. We want our kids to live in this place of freedom as well.

God whispers such excellent answers for the big problems our kids face. As a mom, we must learn to be patient and listen. Remind your children often (especially when they mess up) of their true identity—God's child. If they are not yet saved, explain that Jesus holds the key to sin and it's not a problem anymore. Tell your children in plain words the salvation story. Jesus paid the price for *all* sin—past, present, and future. Jesus makes all things new. Hold your children if you can, and listen to their hearts. Say, "You are dearly loved." Instead of resorting to your old behavior of speaking harsh, condemning words, say a blessing! Assure them that you will *always* love them, no matter what. You know why? Because that's how Jesus treats all of His children. Soon your children will begin to see themselves as God does, and so will you. Blessing your children with life-giving words is a huge key to their freedom!

Go Deeper:

- Do you understand the true character of God? (The Scriptures tell us that Jesus was the exact representation of the Father.)
- Do you believe that the way Jesus lived and the radical ideas He taught on earth are straight from the heart of God?
- What are some false ideals or actions, contrary to God's Word, that you have placed on your children?
- How can you replace them and ultimately lead your children to freedom?

What's Next?

Read Matthew 5-7 (the teachings of Jesus) and meditate on them.

Ask the Holy Spirit to help you live like Him, then surrender your flesh for His better way.

_____

_____

_____

_____

_____

_____

"" Now the Lord is the Spirit, and where the Spirit of the Lord is, there is freedom. ""

~ 2 Corinthians 3:17

Freedom In Christ

By: Carmen Brown

I adore the freedom of summer! I love setting aside schedules, putting on sundresses and sandals, and enjoying late evenings still full of sunlight! It fills my heart with joy to have more time to enjoy playing at parks, swimming at the pool, and even enjoying a few more ice cream cones than usual with my children! As I enjoy the freedoms of summertime, I am reminded that Christ also offers us freedom that we can walk in all year long! It is the light of Christ that brings true freedom and joy, not only the simple freedoms of summertime.

Did you know that the word "free" is used 56 times in the New Testament? The Bible makes it quite clear that freedom should permeate the life of a believer in Christ. Galatians 5:1 says, "It is for freedom that Christ has set us free. Stand firm, then, and do not let yourselves be burdened again by a yoke of slavery." We are no longer slaves to sin! You are free in Christ! Do you remember who you are or are you still walking as a slave to sin?

Are there sins and disappointments and frustrations weighing you down this summer and keeping you from seeing the freedom that you have in Christ? Keep in mind that "whenever anyone turns to the Lord, the veil is taken away. 17 Now the Lord is the Spirit, and where the Spirit of the Lord is, there is freedom" (2 Corinthians 3:16-17). The Spirit of the Lord is in you if you have turned to Him and believed in Christ as your Savior! Trust Him and enjoy the freedom that comes from walking with Him. You are no longer slaves to sin! Jesus wants to help you kick off the things that are weighing you down like that heavy pair of boots you have put away until next winter.

Use the freedom of summer to relish in the freedom of Christ, for "The Lord is my light and my salvation" (Psalm 27:1a). In the Spirit there is freedom from fear, from anxiety, and from any other sin that so easily entangles, as Hebrews 12:1 reminds us! Remember who you are!

> Therefore, if anyone is in Christ, the new creation has come: The old has gone, the new is here! (2 Corinthians 5:17)

Go Deeper:

• Are you walking in freedom with Christ? What is weighing you down? Humbly pray before the Lord and ask Him to reveal to you any unconfessed sin or any area that you have not surrendered to Him. This can be a very difficult process, but He is with you! He will not leave you nor forsake you (Deuteronomy 31:6). He will walk you into His freedom. Remember that His yoke of obedience is easier and lighter than anything you are holding on to.

What's Next?

Teach your children about the freedom Christ brings as you enjoy your summer together. Use the extra time with them to teach them more about Him by reading the Word with them and teaching them some new songs about the truths of the Word. And as the summer fades back into fall and eventually winter, remind them (and yourself) that the light of Christ will go with them and give them freedom as they learn to walk closer to Him.

Week Nine ~ Day Four

journal

Food for the Soul

Wow! We are at the end of the summer and this wonderful *Wise Woman Stays* summer study! I hope it has refreshed you and inspired you to be an amazing mama and an intentional daughter of the King. I say it's time to celebrate! What better way than with an impressive ice cream cake! This recipe is a piece of cake too! Sorry for the pun, but seriously, like its name, it is certain to impress. Why not gather your family and friends to celebrate all that this summer has meant to you? Use the time to reminisce about all the fun you've had while savoring yummy ice cream. Celebrate all that God has sewn in your hearts and any special memories added to your arsenal of praise these past few months. A praise party for the end of summer will certainly help culminate the season and start off the oncoming school year just right!

IMPRESSIVE ICE CREAM CAKE

By: Rae-Ellen Sanders

Ingredients:

12 ice cream sandwiches, unwrapped but still frozen

1 large container (16 oz.) of frozen whipped topping, divided

1 cup of coarsely chopped chocolate sandwich cookies, about 10-12 cookies

2 tablespoons chocolate syrup

½ cup milk

1 package instant chocolate pudding mix

1 chocolate candy bar or sprinkles

Directions:

1. Chop the sandwich cookies with food chopper/blender or simply by placing in a zipper bag and having a good stress-relieving squeeze. (You didn't realize this was going to be therapeutic, did you? There is even a reward for all of your hard work at the end. Now that is good!)

2. Squeeze chocolate syrup into cookie crumbles; add more if you like. Mix well, creating a thick paste. (This reminds me of the ice cream cakes I had while growing up on the East Coast. How many of you have had the pleasure of delighting in a Carvel ice cream cake? Sigh!)

3. Set aside and make the concentrated pudding mix by adding dry package ingredients to milk and whisking together—consistency will be thick. Combine half of the whipped topping with the milk and pudding mixture until well-blended.

4. Layer 6 ice cream sandwiches on a plate side-by-side, forming a rectangle. Now, spread all that chopped cookie goodness in a layer on top of the ice cream sandwiches. Top with pudding/whipped topping mixture.

5. Place remaining 6 ice cream sandwiches on top.

IMPRESSIVE ICE CREAM CAKE

(Directions Continued):

6. Apply leftover whipped topping to the top and sides of cake with a spatula or a spreader. Don't worry about perfection here. Freeze for 30 minutes prior to serving.

7. Holding the unwrapped chocolate bar, take a cheese knife and slice chocolate in thin shavings on the short side. If done correctly, the chocolate will curl. Spread the curls on top, creating a very gourmet confection. Voila!

At our house, we have changed this up and used blondie ice cream sandwiches, vanilla sandwich cookies, vanilla pudding, and strawberry cheesecake ice cream—it is delicious. Mix it up and be creative. You can't go wrong, and you just might not bake a cake in the summer ever again! Thank goodness too, because who wants to be laboring over an oven in 80-degree weather?! There is always a reason to celebrate!

Summer of Staying
~ Week Ten ~

Dear Sweet Mama,

I just love summertime—the warmth, loose schedule, and long days! As we approach the end of summer and see fall on the horizon, it's easy to dread the impending change—school starting, busy schedules, and cooler weather. I want to encourage you to embrace the next season with excitement and confidence!

Remember what we are told in Ephesians 2:10: "For we are God's handiwork, created in Christ Jesus to do good works, which God prepared in advance for us to do." God has prepared our way—ahead of us—and will equip us appropriately for the next season!

I am about to begin my second year of homeschooling, and this is a feat I never imagined I'd be tasked with! Instead of feeling overwhelmed while preparing for a new school year, I am reminded of God's calling for my life. We all have different paths we are called to walk, and I pray you can stay the course and trust God's way for you, taking His yoke upon you, for it is easy (Matthew 11:28-30).

I find the first eight verses from Psalm 119 in the Message Bible very encouraging too. I recommend reading them and praying for God to give you the strength to embrace whatever challenge comes your way. "You're blessed when you stay on course, walking steadily on the road revealed by God... I'm going to do what you tell me to do" (Psalm 119:1, 8a MSG).

Love and Blessings,
Kristall Willis and the Help Club for Moms Team

> ❝ *We gain strength, and courage, and confidence by each*
> *experience in which we really stop to look fear in the face...*
> *we must do that which we think we cannot.* ❞
>
> ~ Eleanor Roosevelt

Mom Tips

By: Leslie Leonard

"Fear not, for I am with you; be not dismayed, for I am your God; I will strengthen you, I will help you, I will uphold you with my righteous right hand." ~ Isaiah 41:10 (ESV)

The Wise Woman Builds Her Spirit:

- Turn off the television this week. Instead, commit to reading a book, going for a walk, or calling a long lost friend on the phone to catch up.
- Wake up before sunrise one day this week and watch the sun come up. Sit in the quiet and pray Luke 1:78-79 and Romans 13:12. Journal about your experience.

The Wise Woman Loves Her Husband:

- Ask your husband if there are any tasks/errands you can help him with this week to ease his burden. Go about these tasks with a smile and a happy attitude. As always, do this without any expectation of a favor in return.
- Give your husband a free night this week. Let him connect with a friend, get a run in, or clear his head however he needs to. In today's society, the pressure on men is overwhelming. We as wives need to be supportive.

The Wise Woman Loves Her Children:

- If it rains this week, go jump in some puddles. Get wet! Have some fun. See who can make the biggest splash. If it does not rain, go for a nature walk and gather items like sticks, rocks, and pine cones. Come home and make a collage.
- Gather together as a family for nighttime prayer. You can have one person pray for the entire family or you can take turns praying (whatever works for you).

The Wise Woman Cares For Her Home:

- Three days this week, start a load of laundry first thing in the morning. When it finishes washing, move it right the dryer. When the load drys, fold it and put it away immediately. Do not let it sit in the basket or on a chair.
- Spend some time sprucing up your yard. Pull the weeds and trim the trees and bushes. Edge and mow the lawn. Consider planting flowers in your flower beds and in pots on your porch.

> 66 She is clothed with strength and dignity; she can laugh at the days to come. 99
>
> ~ Proverbs 31:25

Enjoying Motherhood

By: Kathryn Egly

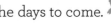

Being a mom is incredible, but it can also be incredibly hard.

I try to get the house picked up before I go to bed at night, but then by 10 a.m., it looks a hurricane swept through. Breakfast is finished, but dishes are piled in the sink, milk is spilled and "sort of" wiped up. I look in the living room, and my four sons have pulled out every pillow and blanket we own to make a fort. I look around at the messy house and feel overwhelmed.

Some thoughts that go through my head:

> I'll never have a clean house.
>
> I'm depressed.
>
> I can't do this.

I give myself about 60 seconds to feel that way, then I *purposefully stop myself*. I *choose* to think different thoughts, and my mood immediately changes.

"I can't do this" is replaced with:

> "I can do all things through Him who gives me strength" (Philippians 4:13).

"I am depressed" is replaced with:

> "This is the day that the Lord has made; let us rejoice and be glad in it" (Psalm 118:24 ESV).

"I'll never have a clean house" is replaced with:

> "Where there are no oxen, the manger is clean, but abundant crops come by the strength of the ox" (Proverbs 14:4 ESV).

I have young children living here, but I *will* eventually have a clean house again. Messes mean *life* is happening here.

I *purposefully choose* gratitude!

I look at the breakfast crumbs and spills and think, "My kids aren't hungry! They have food to eat!"

I look at the pile of pillows and blankets (aka "the fort") in the living room and think, "They are creative! They are playing together!"

Motherhood is a journey; a hard but joy-filled journey in which your life isn't your own anymore. It's about choosing joy even with the mess, the noise, and the lack of free time. It's choosing gratitude when the enemy tells you that you are depressed.

I'm choosing joy one day at a time, sometimes one minute at a time.

Feeling stressed is a *choice!* Joy and gratitude are choices too! *Choose well.*

> Joy does not simply happen to us. We have to choose joy and keep choosing it every day. – Henri Nouwen

Go Deeper:

· Read Proverbs 31:10-31.

· Ask God to help you become a wise and joy-filled mother!

What's Next?

What are you grateful for today? Write down two to five things in your journal and continue to add to that each day. On a hard day, go back and look at all the things that make you smile!

Empower your children to help you around the house! My 3-year-old picks up toys, my 5-year-old unloads the dishwasher, my 8-year-old sweeps and vacuums, and my 10-year-old loads the dishwasher and helps to cook. Our house gets messy very quickly with four boys, but together we can make our home clean again too!

Journal

_____

_____

_____

_____

_____

_____

_____

_____

_____

_____

_____

_____

_____

_____

_____

_____

_____

_____

> **"** Be imitators of me, as I am of Christ. **"**
> ~ 1 Corinthians 11:1 (ESV)

An Example Worth Following

By: Samantha Swanson

Paul was quite bold. He knew that his life reflected Christ, so much so that he encouraged other believers to "be imitators of me, as I am of Christ" (1 Corinthians 11:1 ESV).

It makes me think—is it not the goal of every Christian mother to be able to repeat those words to her children?

To start, I should mention that I don't have kids of my own. However, I *am* a daughter, raised by a strong Christian woman who I call mom. For eighteen years, I lived under her roof, and a whole lot of teaching took place in those eighteen years.

I remember when my mom sat me down to share advice on my future relationships. I know I felt uncomfortable at the time, but looking back, I can see how valuable her words truly were. And by watching my mom interact with my dad, I know that the advice she gave held some weight.

I also remember the times I walked into the living room to see my mom's Bible opened to the book of Proverbs or James (her favorites). She would never guilt me into reading my Bible, but knowing that she took the time to study the Word has inspired me to do so as well.

Looking back on the lessons I've learned from my mom, I see one common theme:

I learned not only by hearing my mother's advice but also by watching her live it out.

In 2 Thessalonians 3:6-10, Paul talks about the example that he left for the believers of that church. He said that if only they would follow his example, they would no longer be in the wrong. They knew what they were supposed to do. They had seen what it looked like in action. It was only a matter of living it out for themselves.

In the same way, you cannot choose the direction of your child's life, but you can be an example of what it looks like to live an authentic life for Christ.

Go Deeper:

- In what ways are you currently reflecting Christ to your children? In what ways could you improve?

- Who in your life would you describe as an "authentic Christian"? What makes him or her authentic, and how can you imitate that person's example?

What's Next?

"Be imitators of me, as I am of Christ" (1 Corinthians 11:1 ESV). With Paul's words in mind, think of one small thing (within your faith) that you want your children to remember you by when they are grown and out of the house. Maybe you want them to remember the kind way you talked to your husband, the fact that you were available as a listening ear, or the way you approached hard days with joy.

There are so many good options, but choose only one to start. Then, focus on improving that one thing for this next week. Though your children may or may not notice the change right away, one day they will remember how you so beautifully lived out your authentic faith in Christ. They will see the way you loved your family and your Savior. And they will know that to follow Christ, the first step is simply to imitate you.

journal

_____

_____

_____

_____

_____

_____

_____

_____

_____

_____

_____

_____

_____

_____

_____

_____

_____

_____

_____

_____

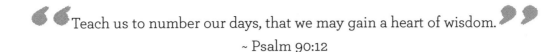

> *"Teach us to number our days, that we may gain a heart of wisdom."*
> ~ Psalm 90:12

Special Time Helps Us Stay Engaged

By: Kristi Valentine

I have the end-of-summer blues! How do the delightful days of June and July disappear so quickly into school shopping time? Transitioning from carefree days at the lake or pool with my kids to the weighty demands of school supplies, new clothes, and carpool schedules makes me very stressed.

After a lot of soul searching, I realized that something deep inside me is grieving. I'm painfully aware that the school year robs me of my quality time with my children, with its long hours in the classroom, sports, and homework until bedtime. Next year at this time, my kids will be a little bit taller and one year closer to leaving my home forever. And I'll be older too. Reality sets in that life is flying by.

Psalm 144:4 says, "Our days are like a fleeting shadow." James 4:14 says, "Our life is but a mist that appears for a little while and vanishes." What profound truth!

Struggling to adapt to life's pace during the school year, I've come up with something that helps put my heart at ease about the fleeting days with my children. I call it Special Time.

Simply set the timer for twenty minutes. Then read, run, talk, or play with each one of your children. Let them choose the activity. Play a board game, kick the soccer ball, or leisurely walk to the park together. Be on their agenda! Finally, quickly record your time together in a Special Time journal.

Special Time gives my heart deep satisfaction because I know that I have made my children feel important and sealed into their hearts that they are my priority. Making this time for my children is one of the most meaningful aspects of my life. At the end of each day, I can look back and feel at peace that I prioritized my kids over my cell phone and social media. And Lord-willing, at the end of my eighteen or so years with them, I will say that I wisely chose to number my days with my family while they were still in my home.

Go Deeper:

- How is your relationship with your children? Is your heart fully engaged with them? How are you showing them that you prioritize your relationship with them?

- If the questions above convict your heart, please don't feel guilty. Guilt is not from God. Simply confess your feelings and ask your Heavenly Father to help you know what He wants you to do. Then listen for His still, small voice and obey what He says.

What's Next?

Experts tell us that our calendars and bank accounts unveil what is a priority to us. Matthew 6:21 tells us, "For where your treasure is, there your heart will be also." Have you ever looked through your planner and your bank statement with the intention of discovering where your treasure truly lies? It can be a very eye-opening experience to reveal the idols or misplaced intentions in our lives. You can do this exercise on your own or with your husband. Prayerfully ask God to adjust your priorities according to His perfect plan for you.

Journal

_____
_____
_____
_____
_____
_____
_____
_____
_____
_____
_____
_____
_____
_____
_____
_____
_____
_____
_____
_____
_____
_____
_____

Daily Plan
~ & ~
Weekly Plan
Sheets

Daily Plan

Date:_____

M T W T F S S

Weekly Memory Verse:

"

"

3 Things I am Grateful for Today:

1.

2.

3.

Notes:

6 Most Important List:

1.

2.

3.

4.

5.

6.

Meal Planning:

Breakfast:

Lunch:

Dinner:

Cleaning:

O 15-min. area _____

O 5'0 clock pick-up

Weekly Plan

	Sunday	Monday	Tuesday	Wednesday	Thursday	Friday	Saturday
6:00							
7:00							
8:00							
9:00							
10:00							
11:00							
12:00							
1:00							
2:00							
3:00							
4:00							
5:00							
6:00							
7:00							
8:00							
9:00							
10:00							

Date: _____

M T W T F S S

Weekly Memory Verse:

"

"

3 Things I am Grateful for Today:

1.

2.

3.

Notes:

6 Most Important List:

1.

2.

3.

4.

5.

6.

Meal Planning:

Breakfast:

Lunch:

Dinner:

Cleaning:

O 15-min. area _____

O 5'o clock pick-up

Weekly Plan

	Sunday	Monday	Tuesday	Wednesday	Thursday	Friday	Saturday
6:00							
7:00							
8:00							
9:00							
10:00							
11:00							
12:00							
1:00							
2:00							
3:00							
4:00							
5:00							
6:00							
7:00							
8:00							
9:00							
10:00							

Help Club For Moms is a group of real moms who seek to grow closer to God, closer to our families, and closer to each other. We believe prayer changes everything and God is big enough to help us raise the children with whom God has blessed us.

We focus on digging into God's Word, praying together, and encouraging one another! Through weekly "Mom Tips" and daily "Go Deeper" and "What's Next" sections, the Help Club for Moms helps women take what they are learning about the Lord and apply it to their daily journey as wives and mothers. Our goal is to spread the love of Jesus, inspire women to be the wives and mothers God created us to be and to impact eternity—One mama at a time!

Would you like to be a part of the movement?

Here's how you can get involved in the Help Club for Moms:

- *The Wise Woman Builds, The Wise Woman Cares, The Wise Woman Enjoys, The Wise Woman Knows,* and *The Wise Woman Loves* by Help Club For Moms are available on Amazon.

- Pray for the ministry and the moms in our Help Club Community worldwide—for them to know the love of Jesus and create a Christ-Like atmosphere in their homes.

- Start a Help Club for Moms group at your local church or home. We can help you!

- We are always on the lookout for Titus 2 women who can help mentor our moms through social media and prayer.

- If you are an author, blogger, graphics artist, or social media guru, we need you and your talents at the Help Club!

- We are a 501(c)(3) and all volunteer ministry! Please go to www.HelpClubForMoms.com to help us get God's Word into the hands of moms worldwide!

You can find out more about Help Club for Moms at www.HelpClubForMoms.com and on Facebook and Instagram @HelpClubForMoms.

Cover and book design by: Kristall Willis | KW Designs, LLC | www.kwdesignsco.com

76253290R00075

Made in the USA
San Bernardino, CA
12 May 2018